FARM GIRL

FARM GIRL

Karen Jones Gowen

WiDō Publishing/Salt Lake City

WiDō Publishing
840 S. West Temple
Salt Lake City, Utah 84101
801-280-3671

ISBN : 978-0-9796070-0-4

Photo cover as well as most of the additional black and white photographs in this text are by Julia Marker

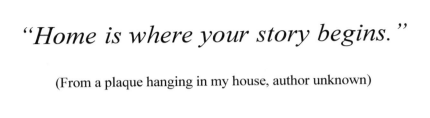

"Home is where your story begins."

(From a plaque hanging in my house, author unknown)

CONTENTS

Illustrations and Photographs

FOREWORD

I want to express my appreciation to my daughter, Karen Gowen, for her interest in my early life and for her skill and effort in writing this book. The part about my life was done entirely by telephone conversations over a period of several weeks. She, in Salt Lake City, would ask me a question to get my memory started; then she wrote on her computer what I, in Aitkin, Minnesota, told her over the telephone. It was a very enjoyable process as she encouraged me to recall happenings I hadn't thought about for years.

It has made me realize more fully how drastically times have changed for children growing up today. Perhaps this will serve a purpose in helping my grandchildren and others understand history a little better as they realize how very different conditions were for my childhood on a Nebraska farm in the 1920's and 1930's than what they experience now. Then, too, how much progress and improvement there was in 1920's farm life compared to the time of my mother's childhood in a sod house on a prairie homestead in the 1880's. After all, history is just the story of people's lives.

To me, my life has been very ordinary and typical of others in our community of that era. It is rather humbling to think that anyone other than family would find much interest in my experiences. Nevertheless, I am thankful to Karen for believing that these memories are worth saving.

Lucille Marker Jones

INTRODUCTION

Since the nearest neighbors lived two miles away, Grandma didn't keep blinds at her windows. The spare bedroom faced east, and a flood of morning sunlight woke me much earlier than I was accustomed. But I didn't mind because it felt so pleasant to lounge in the high old-fashioned bed and remember where I was.

How quiet and peaceful it seemed here without the early traffic noises of city people rushing to work. Instead, I heard the gentle low of cows in the field, the occasional crow of a rooster, and old Pet whinnying for her breakfast. I snuggled up to the great fluffy pillow and lay still, watching a mild breeze play with the yellowed lace curtains–back and forth, in and out–until I had nearly hypnotized myself.

Soon the clattering of pans in the kitchen downstairs warned me that Grandma had started breakfast, and I'd better get up if I wanted my eggs hot and my bacon crisp. The faded linoleum, patterned with large pink roses on a beige background, felt smooth on my feet as I climbed out of bed. I quickly pulled on my shorts and top. The appetizing aroma of frying bacon was beginning to prevail over the usual musty smell of the house.

After breakfast I ran outside into the summer sunshine to explore the farm and see if everything was the same as last year. Grandma's two-story frame house seemed as grey and bent with age as she was. Tall bushy pines and spreading cottonwood trees crowded the sides. Her front yard was like a cool, shady forest, a perfect place to escape from the hot summer winds that blow relentlessly across the Nebraska plains.

I sat on the porch steps, drinking in the tangy pine scent that always reminded me of camping in the Rocky Mountains. A magpie chattered angrily from its perch on the low branch of a cottonwood tree. These brazen birds frightened me because Grandma had said they once swooped down on one of the farm cats and pecked its eyes out. I decided to go around back.

Outside the back door there struggled a patch of heat-singed, windblown grass that gradually thinned out into the well-worn dirt road that led to the barn. As I ran, my feet kicked up dusty smoke signals behind me.

I looked out over the pasture toward the pond. The green meadow rolled forward in dips and hollows and hills just right for running. The cow pond was barely visible from where I stood. It looked like a narrow slit of mirror set in the ground. I knew that between here and there were many inviting patches of buffalo grass, a tender grass that grows short and dense and feels softer on bare feet than the best carpet.

Such are my memories of the farm where my mother was raised and where I spent many summers. The house, barn and outbuildings are gone now. Even the great trees, planted and nurtured so carefully by her father John Marker, have been cut down to make room for crops. A person traveling that road today would see unbroken fields of corn growing where the farmhouse once stood. There would be no clue to the passer-by that here once stood a home, a farmstead, the hub of a hard-working Nebraska farm family.

Yet I can visit that place any time I wish by calling up rich and vivid mind pictures of my summers there. These memories are part of my heritage, the fabric of my personality, and as real to me as the land itself. I can remember the summer visits exploring the farm, riding Pet, the gentle old horse, to the New Virginia Church and back; flying down a hilly dirt road in a little red wagon, then making the steep climb back up to have another turn. In the winter, my sisters and I ice-skated on the pond while our parents built a fire next to the banks for us to warm up and roast hot dogs. We didn't dare let Grandma Marker know about the bonfire, because she was deathly afraid of prairie fires blazing out of control, even in the winter with snow on the ground.

Still, as I grow older, my childhood memories begin to fade and I yearn to somehow revisit the Marker home. For many years, I longed to write a book about my mother's childhood on the farm, to somehow capture the reality of it in print. The few attempts I made were dismal failures, as I realized I knew absolutely nothing about the daily life on a 1920 Nebraska farmstead.

Then while taking a folklore class at Brigham Young University, I learned how to interview and collect information for a folklore study. For one assignment, I interviewed Mother to get her memories of the Dust Bowl days in Nebraska. A folklore study differs from most writing, in that the tale is told in the voice of the individual telling the story, not by the collector. Finally I understood that the story I had always wanted to write must be told in her voice, not mine. *Farm Girl* is written by me as folklore collector rather than by me as author.

I spent many hours collecting the information, typing as Mother opened up her very extensive memory bank. What an exciting endeavor! Finally I was getting the authentic account of the Marker farm, her childhood, the New Virginia community and country school, and a glimpse into her high school years in Lincoln. Even the many aunts, uncles and cousins eventually got straight in my mind and became real characters. Before this, they were unknown, distant relatives who came up now and then in her conversation. Except for Aunt Bernice and Uncle Ford, who were part of our childhood like Grandma Marker and the old farm itself. Best of all, through collecting these memories, I became acquainted with my grandfather John Marker, who died when I was a toddler.

The advantage to this book being *told* by Mother rather than *written* by her, is that when she recalls her early years, she talks like Lucille Marker the Nebraska farm girl; but when she writes, it is Mrs. Jones, the English teacher. Despite the opinion of her senior English teacher, Miss Elsie Cather, my mother is a wonderful writer who clearly and concisely creates a picture with words. However, I wanted her memoir in her true voice as a farm girl rather than that of a highly-educated English teacher. To accomplish this, it was essential that she tell her story rather than write it.

A disadvantage of the telling is that it doesn't come out in a nice, readable narrative form; one's memories don't usually organize themselves like that. It required many more hours of editing and arranging to create a story with a beginning, a middle and an end. And once I was familiar with her voice, I could occasionally depart from my role as collector and take some license as an author, adding here and there to fill in story gaps, yet maintaining the voice of the farm girl, Lucille Marker.

The Endnotes after the text are the dates, facts and additional information Mother provided that might be interesting to a reader but couldn't fit into the narrative.

Julia Marker, Lucille's mother, was a gifted, self-taught artist and writer, evoking emotion and creating an image with words as effectively as she did with brush and canvas. She had been painting for many years when, in 1948, she decided to try writing. She saw how rapidly American life was changing post-World War II, and she wanted to record the story of the Nebraska homesteader as she remembered it.

Julia Marker's written memories and stories of her childhood on the homestead in the 1890's and her life as a farm wife are included in Appendix B, as well as photos of several of her remaining paintings. The entry about the early homesteaders is written from stories told to her by her father Hans Walstad, who came to Nebraska in 1870.

Many thanks to the Wido Publishing team for their extensive skills in printing, designing and editing; and for their willingness to contribute their time and talents to help create this book.

Karen Jones Gowen
February, 2007

THE
HOMESTEADERS

Oil painting of a sod house by Julia Marker

Hans Walstad

CHAPTER ONE
THE WALSTADS

My grandfather Hans Walstad lived alone in a dugout near Farmer's Creek, back when cottonwood, elm and ash trees crowded the banks. Lots of fruit grew near that creek– grapes, plums, chokecherries, berries. Indians would come by his dugout and want tobacco and sugar, and he'd trade with them for buffalo meat and furs. Somehow they communicated, by signs I suppose, because he spoke only Norwegian. He was one of the first settlers to stake a claim in this part of Nebraska.

Hans would have stayed forever as a single man in his dugout because the girl he had loved back in Norway had married another man. Her name was Sofie Maren Stav, and she chose to marry Andre Pederson rather than him. So Hans decided to come to America and homestead in western Nebraska and live by himself in this dugout. He was happy here and had everything he needed. Soon his parents, one brother and three sisters came to the area and settled nearby, so he wasn't at all lonely.

His parents, Jakob and Karen Walstad, left Norway when Karen was 72 and Jakob 67, to be with their children in America. The older couple wanted a log house like they had in Norway rather than a sod house, so they cut logs from the trees along Farmer's Creek and built a house across the draw from Hans.

The young woman, Sofie, who Hans had loved, and her husband Andre Pederson, had been neighbors to the Walstads back in Norway. So many of their friends and neighbors had left for America, and Sofie and Andre decided to come as well. They came in 1865 and settled in Chicago, where Andre found work in an iron mill.

He would carry the hot molten iron in pails and not dare set it down or it would burn through the wooden floor. Two men would carry a large kettle between them, and sometimes their clothes caught fire when they poured the hot metal into the molds. Hundreds of people were employed in this foundry. Andre worked there from 1866 to 1870, when he contracted typhoid fever and died, leaving Sofie with their young son Anton.

Sofie worked as a tailor making men's suits, only missing one day of work, the day her husband died. She was in Chicago when the great fire started in 1872. She lived in an apartment house several blocks from the river. She had all her belongings packed and ready to move out, but the fire didn't cross the river.

That night people paraded up and down the streets, some in their night clothes carrying a single picture, or a looking glass. Half-crazed by fear of the fire, they just picked up anything and left their homes. Some carried bundles. No one knew where to go. The fire had destroyed their homes. The people who were fortunate enough to have their homes spared had to share them with the less fortunate. Two girls lived with Sofie for several years after the fire.

One summer in the early 1870's, before the Great Chicago Fire, it was prophesied that the world would come to an end. People were supposed to meet Jesus in the park at a certain time and should be dressed all in white. It was on a hot, sultry afternoon, clouds were gathering and at the hour Jesus was to be there a rainstorm appeared with great force. Those who had not gone to the park were sure this was the end of the world.

Sofie had not gone, and she tried to comfort people, saying, "This is just a rainstorm, not the end of the world."

Despite all this, Sofie liked living in Chicago and did well at her work, being a talented and capable seamstress. She and Anton lived for several more years in their apartment on 54 West Erie Street. The boy stayed with her when she worked, until he started school. After school, he'd be alone, buying food for dinner with the money his mother left for him on the table. She worried about him home alone, especially after he fell and broke his arm, and she worried that the city wouldn't be a good environment for a boy to grow up without a father.

The summer of 1877, when Anton was eleven, Sofie left for the West, thinking the country would be a better place to bring up her son. She had written to Karen and Jakob Walstad, her former neighbors from Norway, and they invited her and Anton to stay with them out in Nebraska. She and Anton rode the train out with a girl she knew from Chicago. When they reached Hastings, they had to ride the rest of the way with the mail carrier, in the mail wagon.

The mail carrier told her, "Wherever you see smoke coming through the bank is where people live in a dugout."

Hans Walstad lived right across the draw from Jakob and Karen, and now here was the girl he had loved in Norway so many years earlier living at the log house with his parents. They began to keep company again and soon were married.

Hans still lived in his dugout, a cave-like home that was made by digging out the earth in a hill, a bank or raised area on the prairie. These dugouts could be quite comfortable, with a front door and even glass in the windows. Early settlers usually lived first in a dugout, then would build a sod house, and then a frame house when they were able.

His new wife didn't like the dugout, not wanting to live underground like a prairie dog, so she talked Hans into building a sod house. He was so happy to at last have Sofie as his wife, he would do whatever he could to please her. They worked together building the sod house.

The settlers used sod for their houses as trees were not so plentiful. The land had never been tilled, and the many roots from the prairie grass held the soil together. Homesteaders would cut a slab of sod one foot by three feet, laying three of them down like bricks with one foot on the outside and the other end on the inside. The next layer they'd lay the opposite direction with the three foot end out and the one foot in. This made the walls three feet thick, making them very warm in winter and cool in summer. The window sills were so wide that children could sit on them. Some were cemented on the outside and plastered on the inside, so if you didn't know it was a sod house, you couldn't tell. You couldn't see the dirt.

Hans and Sofie raised Anton and had two daughters, Mathilde, the older daughter, and then Julia, born in 1882, who became my mother.

One day in 1896, when my mother was about fourteen, the family's sod house was completely destroyed by a tornado. Here's how it happened. They saw a tornado coming and ran to the storm cave. When it was over, they came out and saw one of their cows upside down on the ground, completely wrapped in twine.

Hans said to his younger daughter, "Go to the sod house and get me a knife."

Julia replied, "There isn't anything left there." The tornado had taken the sod house, leaving only part of the walls.

He said, "Well, then, go get one from the log house."

After the tornado destroyed their home, the family had to live with relatives until they could rebuild. By this time the grandparents, Jakob and Karen, had died and the roof of their log house was gone, so the Walstads couldn't live there.

Eventually, like most homesteaders, Hans and Sofie were able to build a frame house. Finally they had a permanent home and a farm that did well, after surviving many hard years of drought, hailstorms and grasshopper invasions. Then, a few weeks after the older daughter, Mathilde, was married, Hans died. Sofie continued to live on the farm with Anton long after her husband died and both girls had married and left home.

Uncle Anton was a gifted musician who played the accordion. If he heard a song once, he could play it. He would play at dances, although his mother didn't like that, so he wouldn't tell her about the dances.

One time, when he was a young man working as a hired hand, he took ill and lost all the hearing in one ear and most of it in the other, but he could still play his accordion.

Uncle Anton loved to read, especially the newspaper. He took several Norwegian papers and also the Chicago Tribune, and could talk about current events. He'd save the funny papers for me and bring a whole roll of funny papers over to our house. I looked forward to that so much, and I'd lay on the floor reading them for hours.

He never married, because he had a large growth on his forehead that, along with his deafness, made him self-conscious.

My mother would drive our horse and buggy five miles west to see her mother and brother and take them food and things. I remember going along one time and seeing Grandmother Sofie in bed in a little room off the kitchen. She couldn't walk very well when she was older. She was very hunched over because of being gored by a bull years ago and thrown over. It had broken her back, and she just laid on the couch for a long time until she could manage to get around.

Her house smelled stale, like dank coffee, because a pot of coffee sat all day on the stove. Outside was the shed and the old machinery and wagons. Uncle Anton didn't farm but would work for neighboring farmers. The Walstad land was rented out to other people who farmed it. Mother would talk about how she'd like to restore the old farm with a sod barn and a dugout house like her father had lived in. She wanted to recreate a historic place for people to come see.

For awhile, when Uncle Anton was no longer able to care for her, Grandmother lived with us. She couldn't speak English. She'd take my hand and say, "Oh my lieten yenta." She'd show me her finger with a big scar where she'd run a needle through it as a seamstress in Chicago. I was nine when she died. Her casket stayed in our living room, where someone would come and sit all night with it. Neighbors and friends would "sit up with the casket" as a customary service to the family.

She was the only grandmother I knew, because my dad's parents, John and Annie Marker, died before I was born.

Sophie Walstad in front of their frame house

Side porch of the Walstad home

John Wilson Sr., of Winchester, Virginia

CHAPTER TWO
THE MARKERS

The Markers and Wilsons came to Nebraska from Winchester, Virginia along with several other families. George Cather was the first, so the area was called Catherton Township and referred to as the New Virginia Community because of the many homesteaders from that state. However, my grandfather Hans Walstad always maintained that he was there before George Cather.

The youngest boy, Albert, got the Wilson migration started. In Virginia he was working for George Cather and one day just disappeared. He was gone several years, no one knew where.

Then one day he reappeared and told his family about homesteading in Nebraska. He had come out with the George Cathers. Now he had his own place and was proving up his claim, and he talked his brothers into coming out there to homestead. So the Wilson brothers and their brother-in-law John Marker decided to go to Nebraska, to that area called New Virginia.

John and Annie Wilson Marker brought three little children with them and then had seven more in Nebraska. Elizabeth was the oldest, then Tisha who died as a young woman of tuberculosis, and a son Joseph, who died at age two. Then came my dad, also named John. After him, there was Dora, Carrie, Bernice, Albert, Leone and Ford.

Uncle Albert was the rebellious one of the Marker children. When he was sixteen, they were living in their sod house and somehow scraping by. Setting on the porch were a couple barrels of molasses to get them through the year for their sugar. One day my grandmother found a dead cat in the molasses, so they had to pour it all out. Years later Uncle Albert admitted that he'd been the one to tip the lid so the cat could fall in. He'd been scolded for something and was mad, so he stormed out of the house past the molasses barrel and tipped the lid, sticking his fingers in for a lick.

He ran off shortly after and no one knew where, but Omaha seemed to be his headquarters. He tramped around the country riding the railroads, spending his winters in Omaha.

One day in the 1930's, my dad came in and said, "Albert's home."

Uncle Albert said he would stay and help Uncle Ford on the farm, but he insisted on sleeping in the barn. After a couple months, he was gone. Another year he showed up and worked for a few months, then disappeared again.

One time an Omaha hospital called to say Albert died. Ford and Bernice buried him in the family plot at the New Virginia cemetery but refused to get a tombstone. Later, after Ford and Bernice had died, my cousin Cecil Johnson bought a tombstone for Uncle Albert when he ordered the ones for Ford and Bernice.

Uncle Ford and Aunt Leone were the youngest Markers. Aunt Leone and her husband went to Missouri during the drought and bought a farm there. Uncle Ford stayed on the family farm to work the land after the father died in 1904.

Except for Albert who ran off, the Markers were a close-knit group and did what they could to help each other. Even though I was an only child, I had a very large extended family on the Marker and Wilson side–many aunts, uncles and cousins who lived nearby–who liked to get together for family reunions and to visit one another. We always celebrated Christmas with Aunt Dora's family, Uncle Ford and Aunt Bernice.

One summer about 1928, we had a Chevrolet with an open trunk on the back for carrying suitcases. Dad, Mother, Aunt Bernice and I drove that car out to visit Aunt Carrie and Uncle Ed in Greeley, Colorado. They lived on the edge of town, had a big garden and a milk cow. Uncle Ed also raised hogs. He'd go to the lodges in the mountains near Estes Park and get their garbage to feed his hogs. When the hogs got fat, he'd sell them. He bought apples, peaches and cabbage from different farmers and would bring them to Nebraska to sell, usually staying at our place.

Their daughter Gladys, who had Downs Syndrome, was about eight and she kept telling us, "Go back to Nebraska." We disturbed her routine. She always wanted the kitchen cabinets shut and they were open a lot with visitors in the house. She'd scowl at us and say, "Go back to Nebraska," then slam the cupboard doors shut.

Their son Clayton had run away and while we were there, he came back home. He'd been gone awhile, Aunt Carrie didn't know where and oh, how glad she was to see him. She decided to send him to a religious school in Denver that fall. He went there and turned out alright, not like Uncle Albert. He became a metal worker, working with furnaces, and did well in his business, married and raised a family.

On that trip to Greeley, we stayed with Aunt Carrie and Uncle Ed about a week. One day we drove up to the mountains and Clayton and I sat in the trunk of the Chevrolet. Boy, that was fun. He and I had such a good view of the mountains.

As Gladys got older, she lived at home where Aunt Carrie always took care of her. When Carrie died, Uncle Ed had to put Gladys in a home. She was in her twenties when that happened but didn't live very long after that.

Uncle Ford was our closest neighbor, living on the Marker farm one mile west of us. He never married. When school let out for the summer, Aunt Bernice who also never married, would come back from Lincoln where she taught third grade and stay at Ford's. After the Marker parents, John and Annie, had left the sod house, they bought land nearby and built a frame house in 1896. That was where Ford lived up until 1949, when Aunt Bernice retired. Then he built a new house on the same property. Those two, brother and sister, lived there and took care of each other until they died, first Ford then Bernice.

Aunt Bernice, like most of the Markers, saved her money and invested carefully. She had almost $100,000 when she died in 1970.

Young John Marker

LUCILLE MARKER, GRANDDAUGHTER OF HOMESTEADERS

The old farm

The new farm

CHAPTER THREE
THE NEW FARM

As a child, I lived on a new farm in Webster County, Nebraska, near the Kansas border. My parents had lived nearby on a farm with old buildings and a little three-room house, but now that they were expecting a child, my dad built a nice house. He wasn't a carpenter, he had someone else do the work. It cost about $2000 for the house back in 1916. Sears Roebuck would send out books about their houses with floor plans and descriptions. Mother drew her own floor plan based on what she saw in the Sears Roebuck book.

My parents moved there two weeks before I was born in 1917. They kept the old place and hired someone else to work the land. Uncle Ford's farm joined ours, so he and my dad often worked together.

Our farm was eight miles from the closest town, Inavale, which was very small, only 120 population. Our post office was in Inavale, and the mail carrier usually managed to deliver the mail in all kinds of weather, the mail routes being kept in better condition than some of the other roads.

Our house on the farm was two stories plus a basement. In the basement was a pressure tank. Water would run from the windmill into that tank, and from the pressure tank it would be pumped into the bathroom and kitchen. We could flush the toilet, very unusual at that time. Most people didn't have running water in the house or an indoor toilet.

Upstairs in the bathroom was a clothes chute that went down the basement to a basket. Mother had her washing machine down there, an electric one with a ringer. She'd rinse clothes in the big concrete tubs of rinse water, then run them through the ringer and rinse them again if necessary. We hung the clothes out to dry on the heavy wire fence that surrounded the yard. She had a clothesline, but that was outside the yard so she always just hung them on the fence. In the windy Nebraska weather, the clothes dried fast.

The fence had a wide, wire gate that opened for coal to be brought into the coal bin down the basement. We didn't use the coal furnace much, because the kitchen cookstove kept us warm. It used corn cobs and to hold the fire we'd use coal.

We mainly lived in the kitchen during the winter. I had a bed in my parents' room off the kitchen and slept there when I was younger. When I did sleep upstairs, I didn't want to be up there by myself, so Mother would sleep up there with me. I'd dress downstairs and run up to bed, it would be so cold.

For hot water, Dad had an oil heater in the basement that he lit on Saturdays for our baths. One time he lit it and it exploded, catching the kerosene tank on fire. Dad grabbed the burning tank with his bare hands, carrying it up the basement stairs and outside before anything else caught on fire.

His hands had to be completely bandaged, with Arnica salve to help relieve the pain. I'd help Mother change the bandages and saw the skin peeling. He couldn't work for at least two weeks, so Mother had to milk the cows and put the hay out for the animals. Uncle Ford did any other work for Dad during that time.

Under the basement stairway a Lolley engine ran the power to give us electricity. It was a half basement, the other half was just dirt under the house. An area about two feet high under the floor joist and the finished basement, Mother used for storage of boards, old dishes and pans, things she didn't want to throw away. She hid it with a curtain, so we always called that area "under the curtain."

One thing about our house different from most farm-houses was a tunnel going from the basement to a storm cave. In case of a tornado, you could get to the storm cave from the outside or through the tunnel. When Mother was a little girl, her family's sod house was destroyed by a tor-nado, so she always feared them and wanted us to be able to get to safety quickly.

One half of the storm cave had a lot of glass-sided bat-teries, about six inches wide and ten inches long, full of liquid, to store the electricity from the Lolley engine. Af-ter about fifteen years, the engine wore out, then my dad put a wind charger on top of the granary, and that charged the batteries and ran the electricity.

Aunt Bernice, one of my dad's sisters, had an Electrolux refrigerator that ran on kerosene. Mother wanted one of those so badly, but they cost $350, a lot of money back then, and my dad didn't think it was worth it. We had 32V electricity that ran a fan, washing machine, lights and a radio, but it wasn't enough for a refrigerator. Instead, we used an ice box. Finally, in 1950, Mother got the 120V electricity when the REA lines were built through our rural area, and she bought an electric refrigerator.

The first car I remember was a Hupmobile touring car with a canvas top and no windows, just open on the sides. In the winter my father would snap on canvas curtains with ising glass windows so the driver and passengers could see out. Those curtains helped to keep out most of the rain, wind or snow. For real cold weather we kept a bearskin in the back seat to put over our legs for long drives, like to Red Cloud fourteen miles away.

The speed limit was 45 miles per hour, but on the dirt country roads my father only drove 20-25 mph if they were dry. When it rained, the roads turned to mud and became slippery, then Dad put chains on the wheels and drove even more slowly. We tried never to drive on muddy roads or go anyplace if it looked like rain. More than once the car slipped into a ditch on one of the hilly roads close to home. If my parents couldn't get it out, we'd walk home, then Dad took a team of horses and equipment back to pull the car out of the ditch.

On rare occasions, maybe two times a year, we drove to Hastings forty miles away, the biggest town anywhere near us, population about 10,000. Sometimes my parents needed to see the eye doctor there; or if Aunt Bernice was coming in from Lincoln on the train or the bus, we went to pick her up at the station. Once in a long while, during the winter when there wasn't much farm work and if the weather was good, my parents and I would drive to Hastings just for fun, to spend the day.

We left early in the morning as it took over an hour to drive there. On the way we crossed over the Oregon Trail that so many covered wagons traveled back in the early 1800's. I saw the old wagon wheel ruts crossing a pasture and thought about the hardships and adventures of those early travelers. Another place we passed was the fancy home of the man who had invented Kool-Aid.

One thing I liked about going to Hastings was eating in a restaurant. One restaurant had meals for forty cents. Another time when I was about six or seven, we went to a cafeteria where we picked up the food we wanted. Dad was ahead of me and Mother behind me. I liked everything I saw and filled my tray with lots of things. My dad just laughed and let me take whatever I wanted. Mother knew I had more than I could eat, so she didn't take much. I took about a dollar's worth of food, more than my dad had. I ate only a small portion, so Mother had plenty after all.

One winter we drove to Hastings with the side curtains on our Hupmobile. A cousin, Mildred Lutz, came along. On the way home, driving through the little town of Holstein, the sun shone in my dad's eyes and he didn't see a car turning in front of him. We collided and I ended up on the floor. Mildred would have been thrown out, but she got caught between the side curtains and the car. No one was hurt, just shaken up, because we were going so slowly, and soon we were on our way again.

When I was three, Dad and Uncle Ford dug a big hole back of the shop and were putting cement in. Ford was shoveling and I got in his way, wanting to see what they were doing like I always did, and the scoop shovel hit me right above the eye and cut a big gash.

They were building a cement foundation for the ice house. The foundation went two feet above ground, then a frame over that, with a door in one end. The door opened on the enclosed end where the frame was taller and went to a point.

In the winter when the ice got deep on the pond, Dad and Ford would cut ice and load it on the horse-drawn wagon, insulated by straw. They'd layer the ice and straw in the ice house clear up to the top, then heap it with gunny sacks and straw. All summer we'd have that ice. Mother would go out there with the wheelbarrow to get a block of ice for the refrigerator, or ice box, on the back porch.

One time Dad and Uncle Ford got the idea that snow would work just as well. They got snow that was heaped up along the banks and shoveled it into the ice house, with straw all around it. Then Mother shoveled snow into a gunny sack and put it in the ice box. She eventually moved the ice box from the back porch to the basement because the snow was messier than the ice.

When we wanted to freeze ice cream, we'd just scoop the snow into the ice cream freezer along with the salt. You wouldn't have to break it up like you did the ice. Once they decided on snow, they always used snow.

Mother had to work pretty hard to get that snow out of the ice house, especially when it would get down deep near the end of summer, but she would do it without any help. She took great pride in being strong and able to lift heavy things. She could lift a fifty pound sack of sugar and carry it down the basement. She was nearly as tall as my dad, but pretty, too, with lots of reddish-gold hair piled on her head.

My dad's hair was black and thick. I had dark hair like my dad but no curls. My hair was straight as a stick, and I wore it cut to chin-length with bangs that went across. I never thought I was pretty, but that didn't bother me. I was too busy playing or helping my dad to worry about how I looked. My parents had made this farm where we had a comfortable home and everything we needed. I felt like they could do anything.

I was born at home at that new farm house, the doctor coming from Campbell. He had a nurse with him, and my parents had her stay two weeks to help take care of Mother and me. I was nearly two months old before I was named, because my parents couldn't decide.

Dad wanted to name me Peggy, but Mother didn't like that saying, "The other children will call her 'Piggy' in school."

So Dad said, "Well, name her whatever you want then."

Mother couldn't decide until quite a bit later, then she saw the name Lucille in a book and decided to name me that. Edna was given as the first name and Lucille the second, but I was always called Lucille. I never liked the name Edna, although I liked the fact that my initials spelled "ELM," a nice, strong, beautiful tree.

When I was twenty-one and attending the University of Nebraska, often when walking home, I'd go by way of the main floor of the Nebraska State Capitol Building past an office that said "Birth Certificates." One day I decided to stop there and see if I could look up my birth certificate. I told the secretary my name, but she couldn't find it.

She said, "Come look for it yourself," and as I was searching through the file, I saw a birth certificate with the name "Baby Girl Marker" with my parents' names on it.

I took a pen and wrote my name, Edna Lucille Marker, on my own birth certificate.

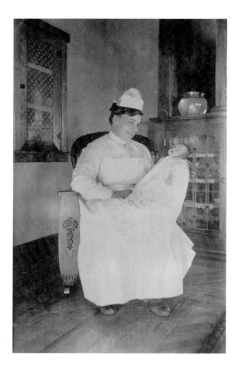

Baby Lucille held by the nurse who came to help

Self portrait of Julia Walstad, 1910

CHAPTER FOUR
MOTHER AND ME

Mother was very ambitious. She often had the recurring dream of flying, with everyone watching her and wondering how she did it. She wasn't a very social person, expressing herself mainly through writing and art. When I was in eighth grade, one girl at school had a paint-by-number set, and that's what I wanted. When we went to town, I got one but never finished it.

When I was living in Lincoln, Mother wrote that she finished my painting, liked it and bought another one. And that started her painting again.

Her cousin Telia Erickson lived about three miles away and did oil painting. Mother watched her and talked to her about it. She bought the kind of board and canvas that Telia used and started painting.

Mother always worked downstairs in the basement on the small oval table by the coal bin. She said once she had done 2000 paintings, many of them sold through a store in Minnesota.

During the Depression, the Omaha World Herald wrote a big article about Mother trading her paintings all over the country for different things, trading through the mail with people in other states. She often said that her paintings hung in every state in the nation.

At first she bought her boards from an art company in Chicago and her canvas mounted on frames. Then she thought, Why pay all that money, I can do this myself. She cut the wood, making the frames the size she wanted, then nailed canvas on the frames with a certain glue to process it. She worked in the shop across from the ice house. When the canvas dried, she'd take it down the basement and paint on it.

Mother figured out how to do a lot of things herself. She never doubted her ability to do anything.

But Mother didn't know much about children. She didn't really want any and wasn't happy when she found out I was coming. She wanted time to paint and do photography and other projects and not be bothered with children.

Dad was the third oldest in his family, so he had five or six younger than him. He practically raised Ford, who was fifteen years younger. As a young man out doing the farm work, Dad would have little Ford on his lap, riding with him on the horse- drawn machinery. He loved children and knew all about raising them.

But Mother treated me fine and we had fun together.

When I was real small she made a little table and covered it with oil cloth. This little table set under the window in the kitchen, and I'd sit there to eat and feed my dolls. Mother made clothes for my dolls, for my one boy doll she made a little pair of denim overalls just like every farm boy wore back then. She made all my clothes. She had an old sewing machine with a door that would shut. When I was little, I liked to hide behind that door.

Every so often salesmen would come to the house, and one time one came in selling Singer sewing machines. Mother bought that and they took her old one with the cabinet. The new one didn't have nice wood sides or a wood door in front. These were the kind of machines you ran by pumping the foot pedal, they didn't use electricity. She kept that Singer for as long as I can remember.

Every Sunday Mother cooked a big dinner and invited Uncle Ford. We'd have chicken or roast, with cake or pie for dessert. She made one dessert called prune pig. She rolled the dough flat, laid pitted prunes on it, then rolled it up like a jelly roll. She wrapped it in a dish towel and steamed it. It came out like a soft, white jelly roll. Mother didn't make many Norwegian dishes, but she did make that.

In the Norwegian community someone would always get dried cod, or lutefisk, as hard as a board and three feet long, six or eight inches wide. Mother brought home lutefisk from the Norwegian community when her mother or Uncle Anton were still alive, because they liked it. She'd soak it in lye water until thick and oh, how it would stink. When cooked, it tasted just like it smelled. Dad didn't like it, so after her mother and brother died, she no longer made lutefisk.

Paap was bread broken onto a bowl, and Mother would heat milk with a little flour to thicken it, then pour the milk over the bread and sprinkle nutmeg on it. I liked this for breakfast. It was good made with homemade bread. We'd often have pancakes and sausage for breakfast, or fried or boiled eggs. We didn't have toasters in those days, but she could toast bread in the oven. Sometimes she bought Karo syrup for pancakes, or she'd make her own syrup with sugar and water.

She used to make cottage cheese. We always milked two cows, and there was a separator by the milk house. She would separate the cream and feed the skim milk to the hogs or chickens. She'd set some whole milk back on the cookstove, where it would get firm. Uncle Anton called that clabber, he ate that and thought it was so good. Mother liked the clabber, too, but I didn't care for it. She used the clabber to make cottage cheese.

We made our own ice cream using milk that still had the cream. Mother baked cookies, cakes, pies, and we'd also have canned fruit for dessert. She kept Nestle's cocoa powder to mix with milk, because that's the only way I'd drink milk except for when Dad milked the cows.

I had a big tin cup that I took out at milking time, and Dad would squirt the milk right into my cup. I always wanted to be around when my Dad milked. I'd take what we called "the dish," a pan with a lid and sides, and I'd fill it with milk to set by the barn for the cats. We had thirteen cats, and they'd meow and meow when they saw me coming with the dish.

At the house we'd throw stuff out back for the cats, and they'd sit on the back step meowing, waiting for us to throw something out. Mother never let the cats in. A time or two I'd sneak a kitten in, but she always found out and made me take it right back out.

Once there was a mouse in the kitchen, and Mother caught it with its tail under a board.

She said, "Go get a cat."

I brought one in, but it was so scared to be in the house, in unfamiliar territory, he didn't pay any attention to the mouse. Mother picked the mouse up by its tail and threw it out back so the cats could get it.

We always had a big garden and raised tomatoes, onions, carrots, green beans, corn and potatoes. The onions, carrots and potatoes went into bins in the cave and we'd eat them all winter. By spring we were eating pretty shriveled little potatoes.

We always raised watermelons, too. One year we had such a good crop, Dad put them in the wagon insulated by hay, and we ate watermelon until Thanksgiving.

In the cave would be big round crocks of sauerkraut Mother made during the summer, and dill pickles, sometimes ham or salt pork. There were shelves full of quart and half gallon jars with corn, beans, tomatoes, cherries, peaches.

To make sauerkraut, she had this long board about eight inches wide and 2 ½ feet across with two metal pieces that she'd slide the cabbage across and slice it, sliding it again and again until the cabbage was all sliced up. She put the sliced, raw cabbage in a twenty gallon crock jar, poured water over it and set the crock down the basement, weighting the top of the sauerkraut with a plate and a rock on top, then another plate or lid on the top of the crock so bugs wouldn't get in. You didn't add vinegar because it made its own as it fermented.

It stayed down there all winter, and it would be at least a month before it was ready. The cabbage would be limp and fermented, and Mother would heat it up to serve as a side dish with our canned meat.

Mother would cook the meat from butchering and put it in jars, processing it in the boiler for about an hour. We ate a lot of canned meat. When we went to town, our treat was bologna in a ring and crackers. Coming home from town, Mother sliced the bologna to eat with crackers. I thought bologna was so good and such a treat.

One time when I was living in Lincoln, a friend from high school came home with me and tried our canned meat.

She said, "How can you think bologna is good when you have this delicious canned meat?"

Dad and Uncle Ford kept hogs and always butchered a hog in the fall. I couldn't stand to see the killing but I liked to be there afterward. They had a barrel full of hot water, and they'd stick that hog into the hot water after they killed it. A pulley was attached to the hog that kept it right at working height so they could gut it. I liked to watch the insides of the animal, I always stayed close and watched when they had it hanging by the pulley.

When I went to high school and studied physiology, I could remember about the intestines, heart and liver and got high grades in that subject.

We'd eat the heart and liver first. The other meat had to hang for a few days before you could eat it. Mother cut and fried the liver, and of course Uncle Ford got some to take home. She boiled the heart and sliced the meat off and we ate that with bread or crackers. We ate beef brains but not pork brains. Brains were cut, rolled in flour or bread crumbs, and fried. We never got tired of meat, we ate it three times a day.

One chilly day in November, I saw all the cats lying next to the barn in the sunshine, their paws crossed in front of them so contentedly, watching the butchering.

The next two days Dad and Ford cut off all the fat meat and Mother cooked lard. The skin would be put in the oven to bake for cracklings. Boiling the fat would be so danger-ous. You'd boil it on the stove until it came to a certain temperature, and still boiling, it had to be strained then poured into jars.

One time my cousin Edna Wilson got in the way when her mother was pouring lard, and it spilled on her neck and shoulders. She had terrible scars from that. I had to stay out of the way when Mother cooked lard. I'd play outside with the dogs and cats, and throw the ball up against the barn and catch it, seeing how many times out of a hundred I could catch it.

One of my jobs was getting the cobs for the cookstove. The corn would get shelled with a shelling machine, the grain running out one side into a wagon and the cobs out the other. We had a big, wire fence woven into a circle that held the cob pile. Those cobs were really important because that's what we burned in our cook stove.

I'd bring in cobs to put in the cob box between the stove and the wall, and they were right there ready to be burned. We used cobs all winter, and if we wanted to hold the fire when it was real cold, we had coal in the basement coalbin. We used everything we had, didn't waste anything.

What we didn't eat, we gave to the pigs and the chickens. I often gathered the eggs in a bucket and put them in the basement landing, where Mother sorted and divided them into the egg case, a box with folding cardboard dividers. One egg went in each division. You weren't supposed to wash them because water would weaken the shells, but you could use a vinegar solution. Mother would wipe them with a cloth dampened in that solution to clean off the spots.

She had two egg cases, one held fifteen dozen and the other had two sides and held thirty dozen. Each case had several layers with a divider between each layer, a lid over the top and handles on the sides. About once a week she took them into town to sell or trade to Schneibers or Waldo's store in Inavale.

Poor Mrs. Waldo was in a wheelchair with arthritis, her joints so stiff she couldn't stand. Mrs. Waldo sat and took out the eggs, then Mother brought the empty crate home for next time. The store gave two cents more a dozen for eggs on trade, so Mother chose to trade her eggs for groceries. Her list had few variations–flour, sugar, Karo syrup, bologna, crackers, salt, coffee, baking powder, vanilla, Nestle's drink mix. If I had money I'd buy candy, but she never bought it.

Norma Lambrecht's mother had even more chickens than us, and Mrs. Lambrecht traded her eggs for good things to put in Norma's school lunches. Things like bought bread, chocolate cookies and bananas.

Mother never did that, saying, "It's not worth it, I can make bread and cookies for less than that."

Once in awhile Dad went to the Amboy mill east of Red Cloud. There was a stream of water where the mill was built, a little dam where the water would go over the wheel to run the mill. Dad occasionally took wheat there to exchange for flour, but more often Mother bought a sack of flour in town.

One of my jobs was feeding the chickens. I'd get a bucket with oats or chicken feed, start at the hen house and throw the feed on the ground. The hens would come out and eat, pecking at the ground. I'd go toward the barn and all the way to the windmill, throwing out their food along the way. You couldn't put it in a pile, you had to spread it around so the chickens could get at it because there were so many chickens, usually over a hundred. Every day I gave them about a half gallon of food, in addition to what Mother kept for them in a trough.

Anything that was work lost my interest pretty fast, especially if it was in the house. I had one drawer in my parent's dresser in the bedroom off the kitchen. We always had the door to that bedroom open, and it stayed warm so I enjoyed playing there. One time I decided to clean out my drawer, so I dumped everything out on the floor.

When I started whining to Mother about the mess, she said, "You go out to play, I'll finish it up."

I can remember starting to cook something, maybe cookies or a cake, and when I'd have problems with it, she would tell me to run off and play and she'd finish it. She had worked so hard as a child, and she didn't want me to have to work much.

When I was four or five, we went to our neighbors and they had a whole lot of eggs on a string– chicken, duck, bird eggs. I thought, oh, that's interesting, I'd like to do that.

So the next day I went out to our hen house to gather eggs for my project. I hit them to make the holes, and the whole egg would break. I broke a dozen eggs trying to get the holes in each end. Mother came out and scolded me, and I ran away from her, out through the trees to the field where Dad was working with the horses.

I cried, "Mother is after me because I broke eggs."

He sat me on his lap and laughed at that funny picture, me breaking eggs and Mother chasing me out to the field. When I calmed down, he explained that the eggs were valuable, she traded them for groceries, and if I wanted to make holes in them, I should talk to her. She'd show me how to do it, and then she could use the contents for cooking. He talked to me as he did a couple rounds in the field.

I felt so secure and peaceful being comforted in my dad's arms while the horses took us round and round. After awhile, when it was time for the noon meal, he brought me in.

Later I learned how to punch holes in eggs. You hold the egg over a bowl, and with an ice pick you make the hole by pressing the sharp end gently against the ends of the egg. Then you blow it out over the bowl. Once I learned, I wasn't interested any more. I remember stringing the eggs up once and being disappointed in how they looked, so I never tried it again.

Lucille with her playmates

Cousin Catherine

CHAPTER FIVE
MY PRETTY COUSIN CATHERINE

My dad's older sister, Aunt Elizabeth, married a carpenter, William May, and moved to Lincoln. There he built a beautiful two-story home, and although they wanted to have children, they never could. When Aunt Elizabeth was fifty, they adopted a nine-month-old baby and named her Catherine.

She was such a pretty little tot. One time Dad, Mother and I went to Sutton, Nebraska for a Marker family reunion. All the Markers drove out to a park in Sutton every other year for a picnic and family reunion. Catherine was about four years old then, with long, reddish-brown curls and big, brown eyes. Oh, she was a beautiful child. I was about six or seven, scrawny with straight brown hair and not at all pretty like my little cousin.

Aunt Elizabeth, Catherine's mother, had a cherry tree in her back yard, and she brought sugared cherries to that reunion. Oh, they were delicious. I'd never eaten cherries that way and they were so good.

At another one of our Sutton reunions, when Catherine was eight and I was eleven, she and I kept singing a little ditty she'd heard, "Al Smith, Al Smith, he's my man, Herbert Hoover is my garbage can." We sang it all afternoon, entertaining ourselves and the grownups, too. The Markers were Democrats, my father a strong Democrat. He said he always voted for the best man, and the best man was always a Democrat.

At that picnic, we saw a carload of the Larrick family on the way to Lincoln, driving to the University of Nebraska football game, when they played Notre Dame. Shortly after, it started to snow real hard. We hurried and packed things up and left for home. It snowed so hard my dad had to stick his head out the window and wipe off the windshield and to keep stopping to clean it off. It was an awful time driving home against the blinding snow. And cars didn't have heaters then, so it was cold.

Uncle Will, Catherine's dad, died in 1927, and we went to Lincoln for the funeral held in their house. I remember sitting in chairs in their living room, the body laid out there in the casket. There were rows of chairs and lots of people, it was a huge living room and dining room.

After Uncle Will died, Aunt Elizabeth wanted me to come to Lincoln and stay a week and go to Bible School with Catherine. Then after Bible School, since Aunt Bernice would be driving home for the summer, I would go back with her. I was just eleven and that was quite an experience for me to get to stay in Lincoln and go to Bible School with Catherine.

During the summers, Catherine came out to the country with Aunt Bernice. After Uncle Will died, it was hard on Aunt Elizabeth, so Catherine came out for a couple weeks. Each summer after that she stayed a little longer than the one before.

One summer, Aunt Bernice brought a poodle with her, a little white dog with a curly tail. We called him Fluffy. Aunt Bernice and Catherine came over with the dog, and I just fell in love with that little dog. I wanted to keep him. He would chase his tail, going round and round in a circle. Mother, Aunt Bernice, Catherine and I laughed and laughed watching him do that.

When Aunt Bernice took Catherine back to Lincoln, she left Fluffy at our house. He was my dog, so friendly and playful. When we'd come home in the car he'd see us pull up and be so excited. He'd go look for a stick and pick it up in his mouth and stand by the car with the stick in his mouth.

Of course, we always had a dog that ran to get the cows, a shepherd dog, a work dog. Dad would order a dog from a man who lived in Eastern Nebraska, and the dog would come on the train. His name would usually be Shep or Rover.

Dad would say, "Rover, go get the cows," and Rover would run down to the pasture and bite the heels of the cows and bring them up to the barn.

I made friends with those dogs too, but Fluffy was special. He wasn't a work dog, just a play dog, and he belonged to me.

I'd go to the mailbox with Fluffy, Rover, a whole bunch of cats, and a pig. Half a mile to the mailbox with about thirteen pets following me down the lane and back. We had two sets of trees on either side of the hay field. I often took the dogs down to those groves of trees. There I would sit and look at the birds, pet the dogs, and walk around in the "woods."

One time I went down to the furthest woods and the dogs ran ahead barking and barking. They'd found some kind of animal that I'd never seen before, as big as a rabbit with a rat-like tail, a furry animal lying there dead. I picked it up by the tail and carried it home because I wanted my dad to see what it was.

When I was nearly home, I glanced down and saw it curled back staring at me with its beady eyes and snarling teeth. I dropped it and hit it over the head with a stick then took it to my dad.

He said, "Why that's a possum."

He helped me skin it, and I sold the skin for eighty-five cents. We had some skunk skins to take in as well.

There was a big market for skins, for fur coats and fur trimmed hats. I had lots of coats with real fur trim. By the time the skins were tanned, trimmed, and colored, it all looked the same, you didn't know what kind of fur you were wearing. It might be rabbit, skunk or possum. But you could always tell beaver by its feel, so very plush and soft. Aunt Elizabeth had a coat with a beaver collar that felt so nice. Aunt Bernice had a black coat that was entirely sealskin, with a mink collar. Everyone's ambition was to have a sealskin or a mink coat.

One time Catherine came to visit wearing a beautiful red coat and matching hat with fur trim, fur on the hat, the coat collar and the cuffs. Mother admired that so much and was examining it closely. Later she went to town for the material and started making one for me just like it. She never used a pattern, she could just see how something was made and then sew it herself.

Mother was very capable and creative and could do nearly anything she set her mind to. At one time our front porch was open with pillars, and flies would come and bother us when we were on the porch.

Mother talked to Dad about screening it in, and he said, "Oh, no, that can't be done. We don't want to do that."

One morning Mother said to me, "Your dad is going to be gone all day, so you and I are going to town."

I started to say something about it at breakfast, and she kicked me under the table and winked. She didn't want Dad to know.

Mother and I went to town and bought the screen, then she hid it under the curtain in the basement so Dad wouldn't see it.

The next day while he was working in the field, she put the screen up. She was a good carpenter, better than my dad, she'd built a chicken house and a little milk house, and there was a shed at her family home that she'd built. She had it all figured out. She nailed the screen over the top and the sides, with a strip over it, and she put a post in the center to support it. Then she made the door frame and installed the screen door.

Before showing it to my dad, she had it entirely finished with a metal framed couch setting out there.

After the noon meal, she said casually, "You know, John, why don't you come on out to the porch and rest," and that's when he saw it.

That became his favorite room of the house. Every noon he'd come home and either before lunch or after, he'd lie out there and take a nap. He enjoyed it so much and was out there every day. We had a lot of ice cream on that porch, and we entertained a lot of people there.

Mother made me a tent to play in. She used old, three-inch wide floor boards saved from when her family's old house was torn down. She made a wood frame out of the boards and took old canvas seed sacks, sewed them together and nailed them onto those boards. It had a roof, sides, and a door to go in and out. There was a window in the back with screen sewed in, and that was my playhouse. I'd play in there with my dolls, and Catherine and I would play house when she was over.

We had celluloid dolls about two to six inches tall, like plastic, except they didn't have plastic back then. Catherine and I would dress those dolls, cut out scraps of cloth and make little dresses. We used shoe boxes for their cars, with a string to pull them, and we pulled them all around the yard.

Or we'd play Annie Over where we'd throw the ball over the tent to each other. Sometimes the tent was in the south part of the yard over the tunnel area where grass never grew very well. Another time we'd move it next to the front porch on the grassy side, or out in the ash trees outside the yard. Dad had planted a grove of ash trees along the entry road going out to the public road.

Catherine liked to ride horseback and we often rode Flora and Prince. On Sunday afternoons, she and I would hitch Flora up to our old buggy and drive it all around the square mile, the roads out there being laid out in square miles. Sundays were always kind of boring to me, so I liked it when Catherine was there. Mother and Dad would take naps and rest as Dad didn't work on Sunday. We hardly every went anyplace on Sunday, like visiting or to town. We'd go to church in the mornings, then have a big dinner.

Sometimes in the evening they'd say, "Lucille, you go down and get the cows and we'll milk them early and make ice cream."

And we'd eat a gallon of ice cream on the screened-in front porch. Uncle Ford could eat an awful lot of ice cream. He'd start with the dasher and be done with that by the time his bowl was scooped out and ready.

I had a long spoon I liked, an ordinary teaspoon with a long handle. We only had one like that, and it was always my spoon to eat with. Once when Catherine was there, she wanted a spoon like it, but we only had one so I had to give it to her. I decided to make a big deal about a different spoon, and then Catherine wanted that one, and I got my own spoon back. I learned to deal with Catherine that way. There was a side of the tent I liked better, and I did the same thing with the tent.

Like a sister, she helped me learn to deal better with other people. Another cousin sometimes came over, Aunt Leone's daughter Alice, the same age as Catherine, and they didn't get along. I had to be the peacemaker between Alice and Catherine. They were too much alike, both wanting things their way.

One day Catherine and I were sewing our doll clothes and one of us dropped a needle on the bedroom floor. That night my mother stepped on it with her bare feet, and it broke off in her foot. Dad couldn't get it out and it hurt so much that she wanted to go to the doctor and not wait until morning.

Dad and I got the car and took her to Red Cloud. The doctor made her hold her foot still and, without pain killers, he cut around trying to get out the splinter.

Finally he said, "You will have to go where there's an x- ray machine. I can't see where it is."

We went back home with Mother in even more pain. The next day we took her to the other doctor in Red Cloud who had an x- ray machine, and he found the needle and removed it.

From then on, she was often bothered with that sore foot because of how the first doctor had cut so deeply and hurt her so badly. Sometimes it would swell and she would limp.

It taught me the lesson that when you drop something, you have to pick it up.

Threshing time was always a big event. We had oats and wheat to be threshed, and one of our neighbors, Henry Williams, had a threshing machine. He and his sons went all around the neighborhood with their machine. It took a crew of ten to run it.

Mother and Aunt Bernice stayed busy cooking all the food for the crew. That was the only time we had iced tea. We pulled out the table in the dining room to seat ten or twelve. We'd have mashed potatoes and gravy, fried chicken, applesauce, homemade bread, corn, beans, cucumber salad or cabbage slaw, and cakes and pies. And iced tea to drink.

The men went to the field with their horse-drawn hay racks and pitched the shocks of wheat or oats onto the hay wagon, and then came back and pitched them into the threshing machine. The straw blowing out of the machine formed a large straw stack, and out of the other end came the pure grain piled into a truck or wagon, all threshed. When the wagon was full, the horses pulled it away and the men brought another one. The grain had to be shoveled into the grain bin. Catherine and I liked to sit on top of the grain in the wagon as the horses pulled it back to the granary.

My job was to take a jug of fresh water and pull it in my little wagon down to the men. If anyone had an errand that needed doing, I'd do it. I helped dry dishes and put them away.

You fed the men at noon and fed them for supper, too, and brought sandwiches out to the field at three for their break in the afternoon. At seven, you fed them again.

The next day it might be at Uncle Ford's, and Mother and I would go help Aunt Bernice. Dad paid Henry Williams for the machine, but the other men were neighbors and everyone helped each other. I always thought that was a fun time. It was a lot of work for the women, but I just ran errands and didn't do that much work.

Sometimes I washed dishes, but always wanted to clean the sink first. Our kitchen sink was used for everything, and it would get so dirty. Mother cleaned it with coal oil, or kerosene, and I didn't like the smell and didn't want to use that.

One time I found out that you could use Bon Ami, so Mother bought some of that, and I would clean the sink. Sometimes I dusted or swept the floor if I felt like it, but if I whined a little then I wouldn't have to finish.

The screened-in front porch

Dad and daughter dressed for church

CHAPTER SIX
THE BEST DAD IN NEBRASKA

My father was an established cattle farmer when he met my mother, the Norwegian hired girl. Handsome, dark-haired John Marker was quite a catch.

"All the girls were after him," my mother would say proudly.

Mother worked as a hired girl, or live in servant, for Mrs. George Cather, glad to get away from home and make a little money. Back then that was what the immigrant girls did when they got old enough, instead of going on to high school in town. They hired out to wealthier farm families, or to people in Red Cloud, as live- in servants and earned some money to spend on themselves and to help out their families.

My mother had been going with my dad and thought he wasn't coming to see her anymore, so she decided to leave her employment at the Cathers' and move to Omaha. There she worked as a hired girl for awhile, but she was homesick in the city and only stayed a few months.

She was back at home when my dad came over in the buggy and said, "I'd like to have you come to Red Cloud with me. They have wedding rings on sale."

She went with him to Red Cloud, where he bought two wide, gold bands for $5 apiece.

I don't remember ever seeing my parents wear their wedding rings. Mother had arthritis in her hands and for Dad, working hard in the field and with machinery, a ring like that would be in the way.

I have a bracelet that Dad gave Mother. It was a beautiful soft gold, almost pinkish in color, and it felt so rich and satiny, not like hard metal. One time it came unfastened and broke, so she sent it away to get repaired. When it came back, it was a different bracelet, the same design but a hard yellow color, obviously not the same valuable gold.

Mother felt so bad about that. She didn't know what else to do. Out there you don't think about calling the police, there weren't any police. There was a county sheriff, but he wouldn't know what to do. Back then, you didn't believe anyone would do such a thing, you just trusted people.

Mother didn't want me around when she worked, but my dad let me work with him. I always wanted to help him and just waited for what he'd tell me next. I'd put the oats in the barn, one side for the horses, the other side for the cows. In between was an alley, with hay in the corner to take with a pitch fork and put in for the horses. There was a box in each stall for oats. Every horse got a half gallon of oats or more, two horses in each stall, each with their own box. Hay was there for the horses to eat, too.

Dad had four stalls for eight horses, but he never had that many in the barn at one time. Flora was a riding horse,

Doc and Jim were big percheron work horses, one black and one white. They were to pull the plow, the corn planter and the cultivator. Dad had a mule for awhile, in the stall with Pat, another big horse though not a percheron. The far stall was for Prince, who was mainly for riding. I learned to ride on Prince because he was very gentle. Flora was larger and more spirited. I couldn't ride her until I was ten.

I loved it when Dad and Uncle Ford put up hay. The hay mow made up the whole second floor of our barn. The roof went pretty high up so you could stack a lot of hay up there. There was a big hinged door on the south side of the barn, bigger than a garage door. There were pulleys and ropes to let the door down. When we put up hay, Uncle Ford always helped, and he and Dad would have the hay cut and put into piles.

They'd take out the hay rack and pitch the mounds of hay onto that rack. The hay went on top of the sling until the hay rack was partly full. Then they spread another sling over that and put hay on it until it was very high. I liked to ride on top of the hay when the horses pulled it back to the barn.

They'd get the hay rack backed up to the barn door, then drove the horses forward and that tightened the ropes in the barn. The tightening ropes rolled the sling of hay into a big round roll. They kept going until the sling pulled into the hay loft. Dad had some way to trip the sling to make the hay fall into the barn. They did it again and again until both slings were lifted up and the hay dropped into the barn.

The barn was southwest of the windmill, from the barn you'd go a little east to the shop. On the west side of the shop was a big scale built into the ground. On top were bridge planks to make it level, so Dad could drive a wagon full of corn onto the planks to weigh it. Inside a cupboard was the apparatus that did the weighing. They always weighed the wagon empty first, then weighed it with the corn.

When it rained, Dad had a lot to do in the shop. He had an anvil on a wooden stump, and he'd take the bellows and big tongs to hold the heated piece. To sharpen his plow lays, he got it red hot in the forge then pounded it with the sledge hammer to make it thinner, to sharpen it.

An old leather punching bag from when he was young hung inside the roof of the shop. I liked to play with that and punch it. I found all kinds of things to do when my dad worked in the shop. I'd play with his tools, pound nails into a board, and I'd straighten up, picking up all the bolts and putting them in a container. We talked about all sorts of things, about when he was young, what he was planning to do on the farm, about my school.

Sometimes I went with him in the wagon to ride around the fields, through the pasture to cut out cockleburs, thistles and sunflowers. He didn't like sunflowers. He'd take the hoe and we'd chop them down, all the cockleburs, thistles and sunflowers growing wild, to keep the roadway clear.

He often sharpened the parts on the mower. It had a lot of discs, or teeth about three inches wide and long, and down about one inch, screwed onto a long iron bar. He'd have me bring those discs, or teeth, to him as he sat at the sharpener, a big concrete wheel out by the ice house. The wheel went around as he held the disc against it to sharpen it, while pumping the pedal that turned the wheel. Sometimes he sharpened Mother's knives, especially before butchering.

He always had things for me to do. "You run do this or you run do that." He called me his little race horse because

I ran so fast. I learned a lot about machinery by holding tools and helping my dad. When I was in tenth grade, we had a mechanical test in home room, and I got the highest grade out of thirty kids. The teacher couldn't believe a girl had the highest grade on that mechanical test.

Southwest from the house was the windmill. Our well was about two hundred feet deep, and the windmill pumped and pumped to fill the round water tank in the basement. There was a horse tank next to the well and a milk house next to that. You could adjust the windmill to pump water into the horse tank. When I was little, after Dad cleaned that tank out, he let me get on my bathing suit and paddle around in the water. It was about 2½ feet deep and eight feet wide.

There was a hydrant by the windmill, a faucet, and that was the best water ever. A tin cup hung there, but usually I just put my mouth under and drank. We filled the bucket for the chickens from the hydrant.

The windmill had a wooden frame tower and a platform with boards. One time I had the idea to climb up the windmill and sit on the platform next to the wheel. Mother came outside and saw me. She was so worried about me getting up there and falling down, or the windmill turning and knocking me off. She scared me with her fears, so I never tried that again.

That's how it often was with Mother and Dad. She thought I'd get hurt, but Dad would just laugh and say, "Oh she'll be alright."

A wooden platform at the base of the windmill had a removable lid covering a pit about seven feet deep and four feet across that Dad climbed into occasionally to adjust something for the well. There was no water in the pit, it's walls were brick, and you could see salamanders climbing around down there on the walls.

The milk house had a big separator. After Dad milked the cows, Mother took out enough for kitchen use and ran the rest of it through the separator to take the cream off. What was left, the skimmed milk, didn't taste good, so that went to the pigs. We put cream in the churn and made butter. Sometimes in very hot weather we had to crank it a long time to get butter, and Mother and I would take turns churning. No one liked the milk left over after churning, the buttermilk, so the pigs got that, too. A five-gallon pail in the house, our slop bucket, held whatever we didn't want and that went to the pigs.

When the milk cow had a calf, Dad weaned it after the first few weeks and put it in the barn away from the cows. If the mother cow fed her calf, there would be no milk left for us. We'd fill a glass bottle with milk, it was like a pop bottle, with no nipple on it, just open on the end. It was my job to take this bottle and feed the calf. He'd guzzle that right down.

One time I wanted roller skates. The only cement went from the back porch steps to the fence, or if you went to the side basement door, there was a sidewalk. That's where I learned to roller skate. I learned to ice skate, too. I went down to the pond when it was frozen and skated around on that. Dad went down with me to get me started, but neither he nor Mother ever skated. One time we had an ice storm, and I could skate right out on the ground, out in our driveway.

I never had to get up early to do chores. Most farm children had to do a lot of work, farm boys would have to milk the cows and feed the animals early in the mornings, but I never had to do any of that.

I was spoiled. I had things my own way, all kinds of animals to play with, and my dad around all the time. I loved to be with my dad. I never thought of helping him as hard work.

Drinking from a windmill hydrant

Marker 25th wedding anniversary party

CHAPTER SEVEN
THE NEW VIRGINIA COMMUNITY

My father saw to it that we went to church every Sunday. Mother was Norwegian, and she'd just as soon go over to the Lutheran Church in the Norwegian community where she grew up. Her father, Hans Walstad, had helped organize that church, they even met in his home for awhile. Her mother, Sofie Walstad, was Ladies Aid president for years and years. That is where my parents were married and where I was baptized.

But Dad didn't want to drive five miles to go there, you couldn't go straight, you had to go around. This New Virginia Methodist Church was close, so that's where we went.

For awhile, in the earlier years when I was small, the ministers would come out and people would invite them for dinner in their homes. Church lasted until twelve, and someone invited the minister and his wife to dinner afterward.

One Sunday Rev. Scofield was visiting at our house. Mother had chickens that had hatched and they were real tiny, so she had them behind the cookstove. I wanted to show Rev. Scofield the baby chickens so I picked one up, and he was real interested in them.

There was a Rev. Marshal who attended college in Hastings, and one time he brought a Chinese student to church. This Chinese student spoke to the congregation, and what I remember him saying is that it was hard to eat the rice cooked in this country because they put "too many waters in it."

Rev. Marshal had a children's time during church, when he'd have the children come up to the front. He'd tell us a story, sometimes using a chalkboard, and I always liked that. One minister had us sign a pledge not to smoke or to use alcohol, and I signed it. I was about twelve or thirteen, and later that influenced me.

I'd think, "I won't do that because I signed a pledge."

Rev. Bibb was the minister who talked to me, trying to get me to convince my dad to be baptized. None of the Markers were ever baptized. They weren't very religious, and when they first came to Nebraska and the children were born, there wasn't any church here back in the 1870's. Later on when he was older, my dad felt too self-conscious to get in front of everybody and be baptized.

We only had worship service every other Sunday, because the preacher came out from Inavale and served the Inavale church, too. When we didn't have a minister, we just held Sunday school.

I remember Norman Johnson reading the minutes, and it was always about forty, forty-two people to Sunday school. He was elected secretary when he was still a teenager, about eighteen.

Ray Wilson was the Sunday School superintendent for all the time. He'd always try to get someone else but no one else would do it. When it was cold, he'd come up early in the morning to build a fire in the coal furnace in the basement. A steel grate opened into the church, and everyone gathered around the heating grate to warm up. We had opening exercises and singing, then classes.

When I was nineteen, I couldn't get home one weekend because of the rain, and that's when they elected me teacher of the young people's class. It was the class for anyone from thirteen up who wasn't married, regardless of their age.

What a challenge, teaching that class. I started listening to the Spoken Word and the Mormon Tabernacle Choir to get ideas.

I decided to hold a contest to increase our class attendance. I divided the class into two sides, and for a few months, whichever side had the most people in attendance would be the winners. The losers had to entertain the winners at a party and furnish the refreshments.

A few weeks after this announcement, I saw the young people's side full, about thirty-five or forty just in my class. All the young people from the community came and some from neighboring communities as well, because they wanted to come to the party. Parties were a big thing out there. After all, we lived in the country, and there weren't many parties where everyone could come. That contest really got people out to my Sunday School class.

Any parties were usually connected to family events. When my parents had their twenty-fifth wedding anniversary in 1935, they had an open house during the day with a party in the evening for the young people. Mother really wanted me to have that party. It was announced in the New Virginia Church, the Lutheran Church, the Extension Club, as "everyone come" to the open house with a party in the evening for the young people. Word spread around, no invitations were sent out, it was just word of mouth.

Mother prepared food for the open house– sandwiches, cake, homemade ice cream, lemonade and ice tea. The leftover food from the open house we ate at the party that night along with more homemade ice cream.

We played Farmer in the Dell, Skip to my Lou, Ol' Dan Tucker, a lot of games where you had circles where the boys went one way and the girls another, you marched around and wherever you stopped, that person would be your partner, then you and your partner went to the center. Those kinds of games were popular back then, even college students enjoyed them.

Whenever anyone got married, the community had a shivaree and made lots of noise by clanging pans together. There would be cake and other refreshments at the parent's home, which is usually where the weddings took place. The couple would come out after they were married, and everyone played games. Sometimes there were hard feelings if things got out of hand, with people forcing their way into the house.

When I was a child, nobody had insurance, so to help the community, they had something called the 22 Club. Twenty-two people in the neighborhood got together for a party, usually an oyster supper in someone's home, and contributed one dollar. It would be oyster soup made with milk and butter, with oyster crackers. You could buy a gallon of oysters in town, they weren't so expensive back then.

When someone in the 22 Club got sick, the club took money from the treasury and paid the doctor bill. It was like community insurance. When the Drought and Depression started, it was discontinued because even a dollar would be too much for some families.

I went to Epworth League conferences with my New Virginia cousins and to Lutheran League conferences with my cousin Mildred Holt. She lived in the Norwegian community where everyone was Lutheran. Mother and I went over to the Norwegian community for the Norwegian Ladies Aid as well as going to the New Virginia Ladies Aid. For refreshments, when the Ladies Aid was at our house, we'd serve sandwiches and two or three cakes.

Mother's heart was always in the Norwegian Church, even though we went to New Virginia. She had made a painting for the Norwegian Church, a mural on the wall above the altar, a picture of Jesus as a Good Shepherd holding a little lamb and a lamb by His side. That church burned down later and the painting was lost.

At Christmas we drew names at school and gave a present to whoever we drew. Everyone gave a present to the teacher, a handkerchief or something like that. We'd have a little party for the families, and the whole community attended the school program where we'd speak pieces, learn recitations, and have a little play.

Christmas Eve we always had a program at the New Virginia Church where we dramatized the birth of Christ and spoke pieces.

One year Mother made me a gray satin dress out of an old one that she had. I was feeling in the pocket and found a thread to pull on, and I tore the dress where the pocket was. It was a six inch tear, and when I spoke my piece in the program, I had to hold my hand a certain way to cover up the big hole in my dress.

We had a big Christmas tree at the church, who knows where they got it. There would be a lot of presents under it, and I'd always get two, one from the teacher and one from whoever drew my name in Sunday school class.

We had a couple Lambrecht families in the church, the south Lambrechts, the north Lambrechts, and the grandparents. The south Lambrechts had lots of children–Opal, Theola, Margret, and others–and these Lambrecht families celebrated their family Christmas at this party. They exchanged presents and each of the Lambrecht children would get six or eight presents.

I always felt so left out because there I was with two little presents when they had so many. I never liked that. The Brooks' and the Lovejoys and me were the only ones who didn't get a lot of presents.

On Christmas nights Mother, Dad and I attended the program at the Norwegian Church. They had lighted candles on the tree. There weren't as many presents because the families didn't exchange like they did at New Virginia. It was always nice to see their program, but I didn't have a part since it wasn't my community.

New Virginia Methodist Church

Country school children

CHAPTER EIGHT
THE LITTLE COUNTRY SCHOOL

The little country school was a half mile east of the church. The church was on a county road and the school on a private road, off the main county road. John Wilson, my dad's uncle, gave the land for both. For the school, he donated three to five acres, a corner plot. There was plenty of parking, the school building, the outhouses and a little extra space.

I went to first through fourth grade at the original one-room school. A big stove over to one side had a metal circular protective ring around it, about four or five feet high, so kids couldn't get too close and burn themselves. The ring would be warm but not hot like the stove.

The blackboards were on the north wall behind the teacher's desk, covering the entire wall.

My first teacher, Mrs. Davis, stayed at our place. She had gray hair and wore satin dresses and pointed, high heel shoes that laced above her ankles. You never saw people in our neighborhood wearing shoes like that. Those were fancy shoes.

Mrs. Davis, an experienced teacher from Oklahoma, had the idea to start some younger kids in a "Beginners Class." She thought I should start school early at age four and be in this class. I would finish kindergarten, or beginners class, and first grade in one year.

On my first day of school, Mother and Aunt Bernice sat in the back of the room because I didn't want to stay. Then Opal Lambrecht, who was in first grade, came and took my hand, and that made me feel better.

Us beginners sat by the stove where the eighth graders would help us. We often colored, and one day someone had a box of crayons with a beautiful pink crayon. I'd never seen a box of crayons with that shade of pink in it, and I told my mother I had to have crayons with that pink for school. So she bought them for me, and that pink crayon was always the one used up first in my crayon box.

Once when a boy acted up, the teacher made him stand facing the blackboard. She drew a circle on the board and had him stand on his tiptoes with his nose touching inside the circle. When she turned her back to teach a class, he quickly erased the circle and drew one lower so he didn't have to stay on his tiptoes.

We sat two to a desk, and one time I had a boil on my hip where it hurt to sit. Opal Lambrecht, my seat mate, changed seats with me so I could sit with my sore hip hanging off the seat.

In third grade, my seat mate was a new boy named Fay Lovejoy and oh, he was spoiled and kind of filthy-minded. I hated to sit with him. His parents were divorced, he lived with his father, and Fay talked kind of dirty and had bad manners. "I gotta go piss." Or "I gotta sh--." He swore all the time, saying "goddam it."

I didn't like to hear that language. Sometimes the other boys would swear when they were off together, but generally not in school.

But then a lot of the boys were kind of coarse, they were farm boys, and they called things by their common names.

One day a boy told about helping a calf being born that morning, when the dad had to stick his arm into the cow to pull the calf out. Sometimes they told jokes about kind of dirty things, not always farm things. I can still remember some of those jokes, but I don't repeat them.

Fay Lovejoy was only there for part of a year, then he and his dad moved away. I was so glad I didn't have to sit by him anymore. Boys wore their dirty farm overalls to school and sometimes stank like cow manure. But I was used to my dad's dirty overalls and to the smells of farm life. That didn't bother me like Fay Lovejoy's language did.

I always had to wear long underwear folded over under my socks and long cotton socks up to my knees. A bunch of the older girls were talking about not wearing long underwear.

I wanted to be grown up like them, so I said, "Well, I'm not wearing long underwear either."

They didn't believe me, so they took me out by the outhouse and rolled my socks down to see if I had long underwear on.

They all laughed at me. "So much you're not wearing long underwear! What's that?"

I was so embarrassed and never wanted to tell lies after that.

Norma Lambrecht was two years younger than me and oh, she had the best lunches! I'd bring my gallon lunch bucket, a Karo syrup bucket, with a homemade bread and jelly sandwich, a piece of cake, sometimes a thermos with chocolate milk. Or I'd have a boiled egg and some meat wrapped up.

Norma had bought bread and bologna sandwiches, a cookie with marshmallow topping, things her mother bought in town, like bananas. I looked at those lunches so longingly.

That Lambrecht family had a lot of bought things. Norma's mother was younger than mine and maybe she didn't want to bake as much. And they had a lot more chickens than we did, to trade eggs for special things from the store.

The worst lunches belonged to Irving Brooks and his brother and sister. Their mother was very intelligent, directed plays, wrote poetry and read books. They'd have ugly bread, kind of gray and misshapen, and not much else in their lunch pails.

My mother always made nice big, white loaves of bread.

At lunch, the big girls discussed their weekends. "Hey, we went to the dance at the Bohemian hall Saturday night."

The boys talked about horses and cows and helping their fathers. "Dad pulled the hay rack up to the feedlot, and I had to pitch it all by myself."

Once in awhile someone would see a show or a movie and tell everyone about it. That was a big event.

One time Desco Lovejoy brought his cousin, Lawrence Lacour to school to visit. His dad was an evangelist preacher and his mother a Lambrecht. Lawrence was so handsome, with nice features and dark, curly hair, and very nice- mannered, a couple years older than me.

After that, I kept asking about him and hoped he'd visit again.

Outside the school, the fence around the pastures and the north field had thistles piled up about fifteen feet. We'd push them up a little bit and make a cave in there and play house like little girls do. We'd get boards and tree branches to prop up the thistles and have a little cave to play house.

Every now and then, a skunk went in and out through the hole in the foundation under the school. Sometimes in the mornings we smelled a faint skunk smell and knew it was under there. The boys put a trap near the hole in the foundation, and one morning when we got to school, the skunk was caught in the trap.

Francis tickled it with the stick, even though the teacher told him not to. He got sprayed and had to walk home alone, about 2½ miles. Oh, did it stink around there.

One of the older girls had perfume, so the teacher put some on a handkerchief and held that over her nose all day. Our teacher, Alice Whitaker, was a town girl from Red Cloud and not used to all the country things.

In 1926, they built the new school on the same land, while we were still going to school in the old one. The new one had a basement and two rooms on the main floor. They thought they might have ninth grade there but never did. The library was a third room, then there was a coat closet in the entry for the boys and a separate entry and coat closet for the girls. The basement had a furnace and another room for coal. The little ninth grade room had a stage, with folding doors that were almost always open.

The stage was built up about a foot higher than the rest and we'd have programs there.

I started fifth grade in the new building. The seventh and eighth met together, fifth and sixth together, and third and fourth. First and second were together some of the time, but the first graders had to learn to read so their classes were often separate. One teacher taught all the classes. No teacher ever stayed longer than two years, hardly even a whole school year. Sometimes they left to get married or to have a baby. One teacher left early because she couldn't keep discipline.

In fifth and sixth I sat and watched the seventh and eighth graders diagram sentences on the board and do their long division and fractions. Once I finished my work, I listened while the teacher explained lessons to the seventh and eighth graders. By the time I got to seventh, I knew how to do all their work. I loved to work at the blackboard and couldn't wait for a chance to go.

About that time the Mattison kids, Myrna and Dallas, who lived up by Uncle Ford, didn't want to play with me anymore. They were good friends of mine until sixth grade. Myrna played with Theola Lambrecht, and Dallas got to liking Theola. Those three teamed up against me that year and called me names.

Myrna was the worst. She'd sneak up behind me and say something mean, like "Red face!" because I blushed a lot.

Or she'd say "Smarty pants! Smart aleck! Think you're smart don't you?"

Pretty soon I stopped trying to be her friend and just kept away from her. We had been good friends before, but then she wanted to hurt my feelings every chance she got. I never knew what was back of it.

Then the Mattisons moved away, and I was glad. If we'd still been friends, I would have been sorry. I always liked Myrna's brother Dallas, too. He had a round face, a pug nose and light brown hair. Myrna, Dallas and I had played together a lot growing up. The Mattison kids used to drive a cart with a Shetland pony to school in bad weather.

Most kids walked to school. On bad weather my dad took me on horseback, with me riding behind him, over the pasture and over the field, then I'd climb over the fence and run the rest of the way. Hardly ever did any cars come to school, unless there was a special occasion when someone had to leave early and their parents came by in the car to pick them up.

When it snowed we played Fox and Geese. You made a big circle with four crisscrosses in the center, like cutting a pie. In the center you were safe. Someone was the fox and chased everyone on one of the crisscross paths made in the snow. If the fox caught you, then you became a fox and you'd have to help him catch the others. The idea was to make everyone a fox. The winner was the last goose left when the bell rang.

Everybody played these games, the teacher, boys, girls, all ages usually played. Unless there were little ones too small to take part, then they'd play by themselves.

Another snow game was playing angel, making angels in the snow. Boys liked to make big forts and throw snowball fights. We had two fifteen-minute recesses and one hour at noon. There were twenty-six to thirty students all the time I went to school, with eight in my class.

A nice-weather game was hockey played in the dirt with sticks and tin cans. Another one was Pom Pom Pull-away. Kids lined up in two lines, we drew two lines in the dirt, 100 feet apart. The one that was It would call "Pom Pom Pull-away, if you don't run I'll pull you away."

Everyone ran and whoever got caught was It, and they had to help catch the others. The last one caught was the winner. A game similar to that was Jail, where you lined up and had to run. When you got caught you were in jail. You had to go stand inside the square of the windmill, that was jail. The others who were free tried to touch the ones in jail and get them out.

There was farm machinery called discs, that in the spring was run over the ground to break it up for planting. Sometimes they would break or get dull, and then boys brought them to school to use for our bases. They made good baseball bases. They were about 18 inches in diameter, the sharp end would go into the ground so it wouldn't slide.

The windmill at the school pumped water that ran slightly downhill a little ways. One Friday someone left the windmill on and it ran all weekend. The water kept on running down the hill, under the fence, into the pasture, and then down the pasture hill, making a long frozen path about two feet wide.

On Monday recess, we took the discs, even the sharp sides were pretty dull, and sat on them, sliding down that hill on the ice path. Since we had only four base discs, everyone had to take turns. The next day some of the kids brought their sleds to school and we sledded all recess.

On Friday afternoons after recess, we had art or fun time. We did art projects or spell-downs, with everyone lining up to see who could spell the most words right and stay up the longest. Sometimes we had cipher-downs at the blackboard. Two boys in my class, Desco Lovejoy and Irving Brooks, and I would try to beat each other. Whoever got the problem right first stayed at the board until someone else beat them. Sometimes I stayed until the end, sometimes Desco or Irving.

Whenever we had to learn anything new, like the multiplication table, my dad practiced with me at home with a slate or paper and made a game of it. He and Mother had gone to their country schools, Dad in New Virginia and Mother in the Norwegian community. Mother had gone through sixth grade; Dad through the eighth or ninth.

Neither had gone to high school, and they wanted me to get a good education. Sometimes he and I would have our own spell-down. I liked school and always got the top grades in my class, making my dad proud of me. He'd say, "I wish I had four more just like you."

Oil painting by Julia Marker

CHAPTER NINE
OUR CATHER CONNECTIONS

All country school students had to take county exams and pass them in order to go on to high school. You started them in seventh grade, and if you didn't pass, you took them again in eighth. The teacher had samples to test us, then we'd go to the county courthouse in Red Cloud to take the exams, with about 80 or 100 kids from all the country schools in our county. The Webster County superintendent handed out the exams, made up entirely of essay questions, no multiple choice. Multiple choice weren't even considered worthy of an exam back then, because that gives you the answer.

I passed all my exams in seventh grade with the second highest score in the county. The highest score belonged to Annie Pavelka, the granddaughter of Antonia, who Willa Cather had written about in her novel *My Antonia*.

That novel also had another character my family knew, the moneylender Wick Cutter. He was M.R. Bentley who held the mortgage for a time on my grandparents Hans and Sofie Walstads' homestead.

Everyone knew the stories about that ruthless man, how he went after the Scandinavian girls so that his wife couldn't keep any help in the house. And how he was so quick to foreclose on property if the people couldn't pay.

As a girl, my mother always ran and hid when she saw his buggy coming down their lane. Mother said when her parents would see his fancy buggy coming, they'd all go run and hide, parents and children. If anyone was there and couldn't pay, he was heartless, he'd foreclose. So if they were unable to pay, they'd go hide rather than face him and risk foreclosure. If Mother was there alone, she feared facing Mr. Bentley, because he would kind of sidle up to her and want to get ahold of her, pretending like he was such a nice man. He had a bad reputation among the young Scandinavian girls.

If homesteaders were desperate for money, they mortgaged their place. They'd mortgage their farm, then pay it off, then when they needed money again, they'd mortgage it again to whoever would give them the loan. This scoundrel, M.R. Bentley held the mortgage on the Walstad place for awhile, I don't know how long.

My father's parents had to mortgage their farm in the early days, too. On the Marker deed, there are a lot of different names of people it was mortgaged to.

Since Annie Pavelka and I got the two highest grades on the county exams, we became good friends. If Mother, Dad and I went to Red Cloud on a Saturday night, I'd find Annie and we'd walk up and down the streets together.

Mother would go to the grocery store and Dad would find someone to talk to on the street. I'd see Annie someplace in town with her mother, and we'd walk around arm in arm, like girls did back then. We were both in eighth grade, she lived out on a farm north of Red Cloud, in the Bohemian community.

Annie would tell me about everything going on in her family and in her community. Her life seemed so much more exciting than mine. The Bohemian community had dances every Saturday night that anyone could attend. I begged and begged my parents to take me to those dances, even just once.

My dad always laughed and said, "Oh, that's not for us."

My mother agreed with him, and besides she was happier staying home and working on one of her many projects than going out to a social event.

Annie and I always planned to go to a movie and finally one time we got to go. If she saw someone in town she knew she'd tell me about them, and she liked to tell me stories about her family. I was quieter and never thought my family ever did anything exciting or went anywhere interesting. So I liked to hear what other people did.

We talked about our schools and teachers. She was going to high school in Red Cloud, like most of the country students planned to do. I was embarrassed to say I'd be going all the way to Lincoln for high school. No one understood that, even when I explained about my two aunts living there.

They would say, "What do you want to do that for?"

Where my family lived was called the New Virginia community, because people came from Virginia and settled there. George Cather, Willa Cather's uncle, was one of the first settlers, so it was called Catherton Township. My grandmother's brother, Albert Wilson, had worked for George Cather in Virginia, and George came out to Nebraska to homestead. About this time, Albert disappeared from the Wilson farm, and no one knew where he'd gone. Later they found out that he had come out to Nebraska with George Cather. He was only fifteen at the time, his parents wouldn't have let him go, so he just left without telling anyone. In Nebraska, he worked for George Cather for a few years, then he filed a claim, paid his five dollars, and lived on that claim. Albert Wilson lived there awhile, got married, then went back to Virginia to talk his brothers into coming out.

Other families left Virginia for Nebraska as well, a Larrick family, and then Henry Williams came later. All these families and the Cathers made up the New Virginia community in Catherton Township.

When I went back to visit my cousin in Winchester, Virginia in 1939, I attended a party given by Edward Marker's daughter for 4-H. When each one went around giving his or her name, I heard so many familiar names from where we lived in Nebraska. There were Markers, Williams, Cathers, Wilsons and Larricks. I felt right at home.

Willa's father, Charles Cather, brought his family out to Nebraska later, after his brother George had come. The Charles Cathers spent the winter with the Cather parents who lived out in the New Virginia community. Willa was about ten then, she and my dad were the same age, born in 1873, and they were in the same class in the country school. Dad remembered Willa Cather being in his class for one year, when her family was living with the grandparents. Charles Cather tried farming with his dad, but that didn't work out as he didn't like farming, so he moved his family to Red Cloud.

While they were living in the country, one of the Cathers, I believe it was Willa's mother, got awfully sick.

Mrs. Lottie Lambrecht walked over there, across the pasture about a mile and a half, to help take care of Mrs. Cather. Willa never forgot that service.

Later, whenever she was back after a trip, she would come out to see Mrs. Lambrecht and give her a present. One thing Mrs. Lambrecht had was a pretty, fancy silk scarf with flowers on it.

One day Mother and I went up to see Mrs. Lambrecht, and Willa had just left before we arrived. Mrs. Lambrecht showed us the scarf and other gifts she'd received from Miss Cather.

No one around there thought highly of Willa Cather because she was so different, wearing men's clothes. She was supposed to be a lady but she always acted like a man, at least in her earlier years. Aunt Elizabeth had been county superintendent in Red Cloud and knew Willa fairly well. I never heard her say anything, but others thought she was a hermaphrodite, a half-man, half-woman.

I never heard anyone in the area mention her very highly, until a young doctor came to town, to Red Cloud. His wife, Mildred Bennett, was very literate and thrilled about living in the town where the author had grown up. She wrote a book, *The World of Willa Cather*, that helped to raise the status of Willa Cather in the local area.

When one of Willa Cather's books would come out, the community gossiped about who might be in it. My dad had told me about a young man infatuated with a young married woman and they were shot by the husband. Willa put that in one of her books, and my dad remembered the incident well, knew the people involved and when it had happened.

In *One of Ours*, Willa described the George Cather home, and of course, everyone in the New Virginia area was very familiar with that home and with the young man killed in the war portrayed in the book. Willa would change the names, but everyone knew who they were, as she'd keep the stories close to truth. People recognized the characters and loved to gossip about what was in the books, identifying the different characters and happenings.

Despite the high interest and the gossip about her books, they never thought very highly of her, I suppose because she was so different. Now all that has changed, and Willa Cather is big business for Red Cloud. There's a Willa Cather Seminar every spring and people come from all over the world for that. Many tourists out West stop over in Red Cloud because of the famous author. There's the Gift Shop, a museum in the old bank, the house where Charles Cather moved to when they came to Red Cloud. You can get a map and tour places like the New Virginia Church and the George Cather home.

My mother worked for George Cather and his wife Frankie for a couple years before she married my dad. The Cathers had a large farm and a lot of hired hands. Their home, huge and very elaborate for that area, had four or five stories, with a sub-basement, a walk-in basement, a main floor, a second floor and the attic floor. George Cather was quite a wealthy man. I remember him, a dapper old fellow with a big moustache, back when men didn't wear moustaches, the kind that came out and then turned up a bit.

Mother told me about working there, that Mrs. Cather didn't know much about housework. She knew all about flowers and read lots of books. She had girls there to clean house and girls to cook. Back in Virginia they probably had Negroes, and when they came to Nebraska, they hired Scandinavian girls to work for them.

Mother said that one time Frankie Cather didn't know what to have for a meal, as there wasn't any meat ready. They always had milk, bread and eggs, so Mother suggested having French toast. They served French toast to the family and the hired hands, and Mother said Mrs. Cather thought that was such a good idea and so delicious.

In high school, my senior English teacher was Elsie Cather, one of Willa's sisters. Oh, she was hard on me. She didn't care much for anything I wrote and it was in her class that I got to thinking I wasn't a very good writer.

There were two boys in the class whose writing she really admired. Whatever assignments they wrote, she praised so highly and read out loud, or had them read it to the class. She thought they were such good writers. On my work she would just say, "Okay," when she handed it back. I worked so hard in that class to please her and get praise for my writing, but the highest grade I ever got was a "B." I left her class with the idea that I had no writing talent.

Another of Willa's sisters was Jessica Cather, who married the banker Bill Auld. The Aulds lived in a beautiful, large, yellow brick house with white pillars that we saw when we drove into Red Cloud. That house is now the building for the Webster County Historical Society.

They divorced when he left her for a younger woman, and Jessie moved out to California.

Jessie Auld did a program there on my mother's paintings and poetry, then sent me a copy of her talk. It is a beautifully written tribute to my mother:

Julia Marker, 1882-1964
    "She was born of Norwegian parents who came to the United States from Norway during the 1870's to take

up land under the homestead settling act. The Walstad family acquired homestead sites near Campbell, Nebraska, and it was here the two Walstad girls were born and grew up. Mathilde and Julia were brought up much the same as all the farm girls of that time and locality were. Brought up to work diligently both inside the house with its many duties and to help outside when needed. But they differed a bit in their outlook. In fact Julia differed from most all of the girls in that part of the country at that time. She saw the hills and dales, the flowers and birds in their beauty and put it down somehow to keep. She wanted to paint them, to write about them and about happenings in her life.

"Well, it so happened that while her sister Mathilde was working in the home of some very fine people in the nearby town of Riverton, a young artist came to visit there and in cleaning his room she saw his works and all his utensils, his studies and instructions. My how she wanted the instructions for Julia, so while he was out, she copied them and brought them to Julia on her next visit home. So with the purchase of paints and brushes her art lessons began, and on paper and canvas she caught the colors of the sunrise and sunsets, the sunflower and the goldenrod, and all the beauties of the Great Plains.

"She dared to open doors and go through and do the things that stirred within her, do them by herself though she might be jeered for doing them, jeered, not cheered, for to many this seemed a waste of time. Her friends thought her a bit peculiar. But as Will Rogers said, 'Why, friends, we are all peculiar, only in different ways.' Yes, even the best of artistic people have been thought peculiar at one

time or other. I can well remember when Robert Frost was thought very peculiar and his poems adversely criticized, especially his 'The Death of the Hired Man.' But he kept on writing what was in his heart and finally it crept into the hearts of others.

"As Allen Tait, a fine poet and literary critic said, 'Robert Frost helped us to see the old things in a new way, in a new light.' This is what Julia Marker tried to do – just to see the old things, the common things in a new light, as she saw them in her heart."

This was what Jessie wrote about my mother, but it might just as easily have been written about her sister Willa Cather.

Oil painting by Julia Marker

Aunt Bernice in front of Aunt Elizabeth's house

Everett Junior High where Lucille attended ninth grade

CHAPTER TEN
THE BIG CITY

My dad wanted me to have a good education. It was always understood that I'd go to high school in Lincoln and stay with Aunt Elizabeth. Most of my classmates went to high school in Red Cloud and many of the girls worked for their room and board, cleaning house and babysitting.

After Uncle Will died, Aunt Elizabeth didn't have a lot of money, so she took in boarders. She rented out four rooms upstairs; she and Catherine stayed in the bedroom downstairs with a half bath. Dad paid her $25 a month for my room and board, and this way he could help out his sister while Aunt Elizabeth and Aunt Bernice watched out for me.

Aunt Elizabeth had a beautiful, red brick home. Uncle Will had been a carpenter and built this nice house. There were oak floors, a fireplace in the corner of the living room, an open, curved stairway in the front and also a back stairway.

A reclining chair with oak arms and a little footrest sat in the living room. It had been Uncle Will's favorite chair.

I remember him, white-haired and jovial, sitting there with his cigar and talking about the club. He spent a lot of time downtown at the Elks Club.

Aunt Elizabeth had a big dining room with a large round oak pedestal table. We'd sit around the table and eat dinner together. During the school year, Aunt Bernice, who taught third grade in Lincoln, always kept a room at Aunt Elizabeth's, along with her friend, Miss James, also a teacher.

Other boarders were a lady from Pennsylvania going to the University of Nebraska for her Ph.D in psychology, and a man who rode the trains while sorting the mail in the postal car. Then there was me, Aunt Elizabeth and Catherine.

My aunt lit the hot water heater on Tuesdays and Saturdays for our baths. On those days, there would be hot water in the faucets. For a bath any other day, you had to put water in a teakettle on the stove and heat it up yourself.

We each had our own big cloth napkin. We used it for a week, because Aunt Elizabeth only did laundry once a week on Mondays. Everyone put their own napkin ring or clip on their napkins and then placed it in a drawer of the large, oak buffet. I had a sterling silver clip with the letter "M" on it that Aunt Bernice gave me for Christmas. After dinner, I put that clip on my napkin and carefully laid it in the drawer until the next day's dinner.

Aunt Elizabeth was a wonderful cook. I especially liked her mashed potatoes on a platter, the potatoes formed into peaks around the edge of the platter, with creamed hamburger in the center. It looked like a mountain range with a lake of hamburger gravy.

I admired the large platter of white Haviland china. I always wished I could have a set of Haviland china like that. It was made in France, a beautiful, translucent white, with scalloped edges and raised trim. If you held it up to the window, you could see light through it.

She made a dessert called prune pie, with no top crust, that she served cold with whipped cream on the dainty dessert plates. She always served things very nicely with the Haviland china, the big cloth napkins, crystal glasses, and matching silverware.

For breakfast, I liked her poached eggs. She had little metal pans that sat in a rack and she'd steam the eggs in those racks. Coming from the country where eggs were plentiful and common, I never liked eggs until then. At home we always had them fried or boiled, usually Mother fried them with ham or sausage. I had never eaten a poached egg until I lived at Aunt Elizabeth's.

She had a nice big yard and always raised a garden. Back between the garage and the fence line was a chicken house, with eight or ten hens to lay eggs for her cooking.

The address was 1812 A Street, a brick street with street car tracks in the middle. About four every morning, you could hear the milk man driving his horse-drawn wagon.

There was an 8' square little entry porch near the kitchen, and inside the door on the step is where the milk man left the milk. In real cold weather, the milk froze and pushed the cardboard top up. He left small pint bottles of cream and several quarts of milk. She served cream for the coffee and used whipped cream for her cooking. I drank that milk because it was bought milk and came in a bottle. At home I wouldn't touch it unless it had chocolate in it.

While living in Lincoln, I spent a lot of time with Catherine and felt even more like her sister. I was three years older than her, but we liked to do a lot of the same things, like roller skate up and down the Lincoln streets.

One day we skated all the way down to the museum at the University of Nebraska, from A Street to R Street, about thirty blocks. Once there, we took off our skates and visited the museum. I remember seeing a mastodon dinosaur, put together from bones found when they built the high school in Campbell, Nebraska. Since Campbell was only twelve miles from our farm, I was especially interested in that display.

Sometimes we went to the high school and heard a glee club sing in the afternoons. I especially liked the men's glee club, hearing those rich, male voices and seeing them all dressed in their Sunday best, with suits and ties. They performed a lot of Stephen Foster's music, like "My Old Kentucky Home." They sang "Beautiful Dreamer" and such songs that were more traditional than popular.

The Coca-Cola Bottling Company gave out coupons for every A you got in school. I always got a few A's, so Catherine and I would take my coupons down to the bottling company to redeem for bottles of Coke. I hated the taste of it. I thought it tasted like medicine, but my cousin liked it so I'd give my coupons to her.

One time she and I went downtown to a show on Saturday afternoon at the Stuart Theater, a real fancy theater that showed talkies. We saw Abbot and Costello. Before the movie two vaudeville men clowned around to entertain the audience.

One of them said "I'm sorry I'm late, but my little Austin got stuck on a wad of gum."

On the street car home, we were laughing about the movie and having such a good time. Soon after arriving home we got a scolding for acting up in public. Miss James happened to be on that same street car and saw us giggling and talking about the show. She told Aunt Elizabeth that we were being noisy and unlady-like.

Aunt Elizabeth scolded us and said we shouldn't act like that in public, that "girls on a street car should be quiet and not act like they're the only ones there."

My two aunts watched out for me the four years I lived in Lincoln. Aunt Bernice especially was awfully good to me. She let me take her car to go places, and she encouraged me to have social experiences, to go see and do things in the city with other young people.

Once I was invited to a party where you were supposed to bring a boyfriend.

I said, "I can't go, I don't have a boyfriend."

Catherine said, "I have a boyfriend, can I go to the party?"

But of course she couldn't. She wasn't invited and she was only twelve. Aunt Bernice told me to go anyway, she really wanted me to go, and she drove me even though I didn't want to.

I had a terrible time because everyone had a boyfriend but me. They played Spin the Bottle, and there I was with no boyfriend. I didn't want to play the game or be at the party, so I called to come home early.

The kinds of parties I liked were the church parties at Epworth League both in Lincoln and at home. We'd play Old Man Tucker, Skip to my Lou, games like that. We called them folk games. There were lots of Methodist churches in Lincoln, and one time there was a big get-together with all the Methodist youth in the Epworth Leagues, about sixty or seventy young people. We played folk games, sang and had refreshments–sandwiches, cake, lemonade or cocoa if it was wintertime.

Aunt Bernice had a friend named Hazel Smith who stayed at the house in the summers. Her husband was part American Indian, named White Cloud Smith, but everyone called him Cloud. He went around to schools and told dramatized stories about historical figures like Davy Crockett or past U.S. presidents. He also worked as a guide down at the State Capitol Building and showed visitors around, a very handsome man, quite tall with black hair that later went snow white.

Cloud Smith liked the outdoors. When they were at Aunt Elizabeth's, he often went down to Antelope Park and cooked his supper down there, just to be outside.

His wife was his agent and she'd call around to schools and places to get him booked to do his dramatizations. He wrote his own programs and was very good. Hazel and Cloud went all over the country doing these programs about historical characters so school children could learn about history. They would come back in the summer when schools were out and that's when he wrote more programs for the fall.

They had their car rigged up so the front seats could go down for sleeping. They always dressed very nicely, but they slept in their car when they traveled.

One time they were giving programs in New York City, and they went into the Waldorf Astoria Hotel like they were paying guests. They sat in the lobby, ate in the restaurant, used the restrooms, and then at night they went out to their car in the parking lot and slept the night.

My experience going to school in Lincoln and living in the big city taught me a lot. I had always been a kind of shy, quiet country girl who went to school and church, and that was about it. Living at Aunt Elizabeth's opened my eyes to a more sophisticated way of living. Getting acquainted with her boarders introduced me to many different people and ways of life, and having to go to this big high school from my little country school helped me to overcome my shyness.

It is because of my aunts that I learned to speak in front of an audience. When I first started high school, I panicked if I had to stand up and give an oral report. My knees and hands shook the paper and my voice quivered. I changed classes if I found out I'd have to give an oral report.

My aunts wanted Catherine and me to take dramatic lessons from Mrs. Ada Malcolm. Every Saturday morning, we walked the seven blocks to Mrs. Malcolm's house. She gave us students, seven or eight in the class, a poem or story to learn and recite in front of the group. The following week, she suggested how to make the characters and dialogue more real and how to speak more clearly. One piece I learned was "Li'l Brown Baby," by Paul Lawrence Dunbar.

After mastering a recitation, Mrs. Malcolm would have two or three of us go and present at a women's club or some group requesting one of her programs. The first couple of times were agonizing for me, but eventually I began to get compliments and my fear and shyness lessened.

I wanted to be a teacher like Aunt Bernice, so after high school I enrolled in Kearney State Teacher's College to get my teaching certificate. I taught country school during the Depression, and then went back to Lincoln to attend the University of Nebraska. I graduated from the

University in 1940, and that summer traveled to different areas of the country with girlfriends.

I taught Junior High for two years in Scotts Bluff before deciding to pursue a Masters degree in speech at Northwestern University in Chicago. At Northwestern I met Bill Jones, a divinity student at the university. We married in 1944 and lived in central Illinois where he served as a Methodist minister.

We were blessed with four very smart daughters, so my dad got his wish to have "four more just like you."

High School Graduation, 1934

At home on the farm

CHAPTER ELEVEN

THE STOCK MARKET CRASH

I was in Lincoln starting high school in 1929 when the stock market crashed. I didn't even know what the stock market was. I heard that there were businessmen who lost so much money in the stock market that they were jumping out of windows, in places like New York and Chicago.

When an Extra was put out by the newspaper, the newsboys out on the street called, "Extra, extra, read all about it!"

And people came out of their houses to buy a paper and "read all about it."

That's how we got the news of the stock market crashing. It didn't change anything in my life. I still went to school every day and ate dinner every evening in Aunt Elizabeth's dining room.

With all the talk about investors losing everything after the stock market crash, I got to thinking about Deveraux Anderson and his young wife.

One summer when I was about ten, Catherine and I were playing outside in my yard, and a big black Cadillac drove into the farm yard. There were four strange people in the car. Who were these people visiting us in a *Cadillac*? Two very excited little girls ran into the house to tell my mother.

The strange people were from Florida and claimed to be relatives of my dad. They had stopped at Ray Wilson's, who had sent them on to our place. When my dad came in, they explained how they were related, and he was very friendly to them, inviting them to dinner.

Since Mother didn't have anything ready, they said they would go to town and bring something back for the meal. They invited me to ride along, and I sat on a little fold-down seat right in front of the back seat of their big Cadillac.

The visitor's names were Deveraux Anderson and his wife, who owned the car, and Clifton and Minnie Brill. Deveraux and Clifton were cousins and second cousins to my dad. Deveraux and his wife were very lovey-dovey. Sitting in the living room visiting with my parents, she sat on his lap and rubbed his face, acting silly with him and talking babyish. I was fascinated with her because I'd never seen anyone like her, dressed so stylish yet acting so silly. No grownups I knew ever talked or acted like that, not even newlyweds.

On the way to Inavale, Deveraux's wife got very excited and said, "Look, look! There's an eagle! Stop the car Honeybun, I want you to see the big eagle."

He stopped and she pointed to a big bird landing on a telephone pole.

I said, "That's a hawk. We see lots of those around here. They eat the mice in the fields."

When we got to Inavale, they took me into the drug store and gave me two dollars to buy candy! Never in my life had I been able to buy so much candy. I picked out several kinds, some that I liked and some that I knew Catherine liked, and went home with two big bags of yummy candy. I couldn't wait to show Catherine.

The two couples stayed with us a few days. Our round oak dining table was extended with leaves and the white tablecloth stayed on. Meal time was a fascinating event, watching these people who were so different from anyone I'd seen before. Deveraux was a promoter and investor and talked endlessly about the opportunities in Florida to get rich. He wanted my father to give him money to invest. Dad wasn't much interested in that kind of investing. However, Dad did give him $100 when they left, since Deveraux was family and since Dad was afraid they might not make it back to Florida the way he was throwing money around.

In 1929, Deveraux lost everything, and of course he never paid my dad back the $100. We never heard from him again. Minnie and Clifton Brill were more stable, common people and we heard from them often over the years.

When the stock market crashed, I thought about Deveraux and his silly young wife and their big Cadillac, and wondered what became of them.

Back home though, around '31 or '32, my dad didn't get hardly anything for his crops. Corn was selling for five cents a bushel, and he said, "Well, I'm not going to sell my corn for five cents a bushel."

So that year he didn't buy coal like he always did. He just burned the whole cobs of corn in the cookstove and the furnace. He dried them and then burned the cobs, corn and all.

Dad and Uncle Ford used to drive fifteen head or more of cattle down to Inavale eight miles down the road, both men on horseback driving the herd. Close to the railroad tracks and the Inavale depot was a penned off area for the cattle coming in. When the train came in, the men would get the cattle one at a time up a chute into the cattle car. The chute had fences on both sides to keep the cattle in line. Then my dad would ride on the train with the cattle down to market in St. Louis or Kansas City.

One time in 1927 or '28, before the stock market crash, he was so proud because he had topped the market in Kansas City. His cattle had brought $14.98 for 100 lbs., the highest price paid for cattle at that market. Then a few years later, around 1933, cattle were selling for $3.00 for 100 lbs.

Still, my dad had plenty of money, but he wasn't spending it. He didn't want to keep it in the bank after a lot of them closed, so he invested it in different places like bonds or mortgages.

One time he held a mortgage on someone who didn't pay. He'd have me write to them and pretty soon we'd hear back that they were trying, they'd pay as soon as they could. After a period of time, they'd pay. When I was twelve, I had received a bookkeeping set so I could keep track of his accounts and his investments. That really surprised me, because I didn't get birthday presents, or even much for Christmas.

Once when I was seven, I read somewhere, probably in a book at school, about a birthday party where you invited friends and celebrated your birthday. I told Mother that I wanted a birthday party, and she hinted that I might get one. So that year on my birthday, I looked and looked for people to come down our lane, but nobody came. She hadn't invited anyone.

That wasn't mean on her part, because no one we knew ever had birthday parties. The only time I'd heard of them was in books. No one really celebrated birthdays out in our community even before the stock market crashed, you were just a year older. The Depression didn't make any difference with birthdays, or with Christmas either, because children never expected much at those times. Back then children weren't showered with gifts, not even at Christmas. I always got a book from Aunt Bernice and as long as there was Santa Claus, I'd get something from my parents.

One time around Christmas, we were in town and I saw this nice, big beautiful doll that had curly brown hair, a beautiful complexion, and eyes that blinked. She was about two feet tall, and you could move her arms and legs. Oh, how I wanted that doll!

Mother bit her lip and said, "Oh dear, Lucille, look how expensive it is. I don't think you can have that."

Dad laughed and said, "That's not for you, Lucille, it's not worth it."

A few weeks later I was playing in the bedroom next to the kitchen and saw a box under the bed. There was that doll! I didn't say anything, just pushed the box back under the bed.

I got that from Santa Claus on Christmas Day, and that was probably the biggest present I ever received from Santa or anyone.

One Christmas Eve, Dad came in from doing the chores kind of late.

He said, "Better get to bed, I hear some noises out there."

I hung my stocking on the cupboard. Our tree was a few branches from one of our pine trees, stuck in a can of sand. You couldn't go out and cut trees, this was Nebraska farm land, and trees were scarce. And you wouldn't think of buying one.

We'd always celebrate Christmas with the Lutz's, Aunt Dora, Uncle John and their kids. One Christmas Eve they arrived in their car, and it was kind of snowing. We could see Ford and Bernice coming over the hill in their horse-drawn wagon.

Aunt Dora teased them, "All you had was a mile to go, and you had to take the wagon!" Back then, people drove their cars in good weather, but in rain or snow they felt more secure with the horse and wagon.

I'd get a present from the Lutz's, a present from Ford and Bernice, and one from Santa Claus. In my stocking, I'd get candy, an orange, pencils, a necklace or bracelet. One year when Christmas was at the Lutz's, my dad gave me a leather case with a manicure set containing a file, scissors, and a cuticle pusher. I used that for years and years; it was a very useful present.

I always looked forward to getting a book from Aunt Bernice, usually the Bobbsey Twins. I loved to read and always wanted more books to read. I couldn't get books at the Red Cloud library because you could only keep them two weeks, and we weren't sure of getting to town in two weeks. It was a nickel a day if you were overdue. We'd go to Inavale to trade eggs every week, but there was no library there. Just a post office, a bank, a lumberyard, a drug store and the Schneider and Waldo's stores.

While Aunt Bernice was home from Lincoln for her Christmas vacation, Dad and I would go over there and visit in the evenings. Mother didn't go, she preferred to stay home and work on one of her projects.

Dad, Bernice and Ford would talk for hours. Once I was telling Aunt Bernice about our school play, and I gave my part in the recitation as well as everyone else's. I had them all memorized, and she was so tickled by that.

Ford's house was heated by a round hard coal burner with lots of chrome that sat in the middle of the dining room. It had a point on top, glass doors where you could see the red fire, a chrome rack around it so you could sit close to it and put your feet on the rack. I'd sit on the little footstool next to the stove, listening to their conversation, enthralled by Aunt Bernice's stories. And we'd eat candy.

Aunt Bernice always brought lots of candy home at Christmas, chocolate-covered cherries, ribbon-like hard candy, and raspberry candy with soft centers. She would tell us stories about teaching third grade. When it was time for recess, she had her students turn, rise and pass before they went out to play. She would say "turn," and they'd turn in their seats, then "rise," and they'd get up from their seats, and then "pass," and they filed out for recess. Her biggest discipline problems were kids shooting paper wads in class.

One of her students she called "Hoodabooboo," because that was his favorite word. He was mentally deficient and always said "hoodabooboo" about everything. She was trying to teach him something and trying to help him along.

I remember her talking about one little boy who was her favorite. She thought he was such a nice little boy. She told us how well-mannered and polite he was, and such a good student. Then it turned out that this little boy grew up and went to prison. He robbed a bank in southwestern Nebraska and killed seven people. Aunt Bernice could hardly believe it possible, because in third grade he had been the nicest boy. I remember when that happened, reading in the paper about him.

The paper quoted him, "I wish someone had stopped me, I was afraid I was going to kill people."

He said he had tried to get help but no one would listen. I had read in the Bible about demons in people, and it sounded to me like he had a demon. So I thought, maybe there is something to this idea about demons in people. It would explain a lot, especially in a situation like that.

I felt very fortunate in the kind of wholesome life I'd had growing up. Besides our nice farm, we had a network of friends, neighbors and relatives both in the New Virginia and Norwegian communities. I never felt affected much by the stock market crash or the Great Depression, because not that much changed for me. I came home summers and holidays; my life went on as usual.

The hardest part was seeing the hardship on the farmers and their families in our community. First it was the Depression, then the dust storms began, and then it was a long drought when no crops would grow.

The Nebraska farm girl home for the summer

Catherine May

CHAPTER TWELVE
A SAD TALE

Catherine had always been strong-willed, but then something happened that made things worse. She was about thirteen and was playing across the street with a girl her age named Ruthie. I was sitting in the big chair in Aunt Elizabeth's living room, studying and doing homework.

Catherine came through the front door, slamming it shut.

She stomped into the living room, saying, "Ruthie said I'm adopted! I'm not adopted!"

I just looked at her, not knowing what to say. Aunt Elizabeth and Uncle Will weren't able to have children, and they had adopted Catherine when she was nine months old. All the Markers knew, but apparently no one had told her. We never thought anything about it, she was just part of the large Marker family like I was and like all the other cousins.

Aunt Elizabeth took her into the bedroom and had a talk with her. After awhile, Catherine stormed out of the bedroom, her brown eyes flashing, and her cheeks red.

She said, "She's not my real mother, so I don't have to do what she says!"

From then on, Catherine was a problem. She became rebellious and disobedient, even more than before.

Then when she was sixteen, her mother died. Aunt Elizabeth was sixty-six and sitting in her chair on a summer day when she suffered a quick heart attack. Hazel Smith was staying there at the time and called Aunt Bernice out at Uncle Ford's. I was nineteen and hired to teach school that fall, so I wouldn't be in Lincoln to help with Catherine. She became Aunt Bernice's responsibility.

After that, Catherine became a bigger problem. It was up to Aunt Bernice to take care of her, and poor Bernice wasn't equipped for it. After all, she had never married or had any children.

We went up for the funeral and Catherine came home with Aunt Bernice and stayed out in the country with us the rest of the summer.

When they returned to Lincoln in the fall, the two of them lived in the house with a few boarders. Not as many as before, because Aunt Bernice taught school and couldn't do all the cooking and laundry for a lot of boarders. Besides, she had her own money and didn't need to keep boarders for a living like her sister had done.

I was teaching country school by then and Aunt Bernice said, "Oh, Lucille, I wish you were going to be here to help with Catherine."

Two years later, I moved back to Lincoln to attend the University of Nebraska. Catherine went out with a lot of guys and a few girls, and they'd drive around and go to bars. I went along a few times to be with her, to try and watch out for her, but by then she was set in her ways. I didn't like going with them. They were wild and here I was, a non-drinker, because that's how my family was and because I'd signed a pledge at the New Virginia church when I was twelve.

Catherine started at the University of Nebraska, and we all hoped she would get busy with her studies and settle down, but she didn't go to class very often. She liked a guy named Elwin who was twenty-seven, ten years older than her. When she turned eighteen, she married him. He was an established carpenter who had money, and she started wearing fancy clothes, buying herself a raccoon coat.

In the early part of the War, there was an air base in Lincoln, and she got to running around with one of the guys there. She got pregnant by him and divorced Elwin to marry the other. He was from Oregon, and when he went overseas, she went to Oregon to live with his folks.

Through the years, we would hear from Catherine now and then. Not very often. She corresponded most often with Hazel Smith. As time went on, her letters to me and Aunt Bernice came less and less frequently, but Hazel would keep us informed.

Catherine had three boys from this marriage, but eventually they divorced. She had a lot of problems with her boys.

One summer she came out to Nebraska to see Aunt Bernice and Uncle Ford. She wanted them to take on the oldest boy and take care of him, because he was her biggest problem. They said no, and that made her mad. After that, she didn't want anything to do with any of the Markers. She stopped writing to us altogether, and for awhile we only heard about her through Hazel Smith.

She worked as a waitress in Oregon, trying to support herself and her boys. This oldest son eventually got into bad trouble and went to prison. My heart was breaking for Catherine. It didn't matter to me that she was adopted, she was still my family.

I wrote to her and told her how I had enjoyed growing up with her, that she was like a sister to me. I wrote that she had always been such an important part of my life and recalled what fun we always had together. How I treasured those memories! I never heard back from her. She was mad at Aunt Bernice and probably mad at me, too.

When Aunt Bernice died in 1970, she left Catherine $1000. I found her address and wrote again, telling her to contact this particular lawyer, that Aunt Bernice had died. I don't know if she ever did or not. My cousin Cecil Johnson and I each got $25,000 from our aunt, and I felt kind of bad about that. But it was how Catherine had acted.

I never heard from her or learned anything more about her or her boys.

Young Lucille and Catherine in a buggy

CHAPTER THIRTEEN
DUST BOWL DAYS

For us, the Dust Bowl started in 1934. We didn't have any rain that summer, the corn grew up about twelve inches high, then turned brown and fell over. There wasn't enough moisture in the soil to hold it up. It was growing in dust, so it just fell over. There was no snow that winter, or if there was it was very little, didn't amount to anything and blew off the fields.

In March of 1935, I was at Kearney State Teachers College going to school for my rural teaching certificate. Mother and Dad drove up one weekend to bring me home. A girlfriend came, too. Her dad was going to come out from Red Cloud the next day to pick her up at our place.

We approached the house and saw a huge black cloud. My dad hurried and did the chores before the storm came. It was evening, but things were darker than usual because of these clouds and dust blowing everywhere. Mother quickly went in and turned the house lights on, and the yard light on the windmill. There was no rain, just dust and awfully hard wind blowing.

We went to the basement because Mother thought it would be a tornado and, of course, we always went to the cellar for a tornado. My dad hadn't come in yet from the barn and Mother was pretty worried because storms frightened her. The memory of her family's sod house being destroyed by a tornado was still clear in her mind.

Dad didn't come in for the longest time. Finally he made his way in and said he'd gotten lost from the barn. It was dark and blowing dust so hard that he couldn't see at all. He couldn't see the light on the windmill or the lights in the house, and he couldn't tell what direction to go to find the house from the barn. For twenty years, he had taken that path from the barn to the house and probably could have found his way blind-folded. Yet caught in the blackness of swirling dust, he became disoriented and lost in his own yard. Eventually the wind let up a little, enough so he could see the light on the windmill and he was able to find the house. He was completely covered in dirt, just black from head to toe.

In the house, the dust was so thick we had to hold wet handkerchiefs over our faces so we could breathe. We went to bed that night with the sound of the wind howling and dust hitting the windows.

In the morning, my friend and I woke up and looked at each other and started laughing. Our faces were gray, covered in dust. The quilt on my bed had lots of colors and designs on it, but now with the dust covering it so thickly it looked like gray velvet. About a half-inch of very fine dust covered the floors of the house. During the night, the dust had collected around the pig fence so much that it made a drift three feet high, and the pigs walked right over the fence.

We listened to the radio and to the party line telephone to hear news about the storm. There were so many stories about people getting lost during the storm and stranded out on the roads.

We had dirt roads, but the main roads to town had gravel on top. As people drove on them, gravel would build up along the edge of the road and make a raised line or ridge. On the rest of the surface, the gravel would get ground into the dirt until it was pretty much back to being a dirt road, but there would still be this ridge of gravel along the edge.

That night cars stalled with the dust clogging the engines. The storm lasted through the night and people couldn't stay in their cars. So they'd get out and almost crawl along the road following the ridge of gravel at the edge until they could get into Campbell, Inavale or whatever town was closest. A lot of the people said they crawled most of the way, because that was the only way they could tell where the gravel ridge was. They would feel it with their hands because they couldn't see a thing, it was so dark with all the dust blowing.

That was the worst of the dust storms, although we had others and always a lot of dust everywhere all the time. Nebraska is a very windy state anyway. There was a saying back then that when the wind blew from the south it blew our farm over to our neighbors. And then when the wind blows from the north, it will blow our farm back again. Another saying is that Nebraska only has three days of the week, because the wind blows four days out of the week.

Mother finally gave up on beating the rugs and rolled them up and put them away, so we had no rugs on the floor. She took down the curtains because they collected too much dust. In those days, no one in the country had vacuum cleaners because very few homes had electricity. Our electricity was 32V, powered by a windcharger on top of the granary, and there were no 32V vacuum cleaners. Mother did what she could to sweep dust outside with her broom. But a broom doesn't get much dust out of a rug. She took her heavy wool rugs out to hang on the clothesline, beating them over and over to try and get the dust out.

The dust blew like snow and drifted like snow. Unfortunately, it didn't melt like snow. We had a spare bedroom on the northwest corner of the house. One morning Mother and I went in there to clean and found dust piled on the floor at least ten inches high under both the north and the west windows. She sent me to get the bushel bucket and a shovel, and we shoveled the dirt into the bucket and then swept up the rest.

To me, the Dust bowl and the Depression are interrelated, because together they changed things for a lot of families in our community. Before the Depression, our country school teacher was paid $100 a month. Then before the Drought really hit, it dropped down to $45 a month. In 1935, after the Dust Bowl and the Drought started, I got a school and started teaching for $35 a month. That was south of Red Cloud near the Kansas state line. Our community never went that low, only to $40 a month.

A lot of the people in our community were affected, because they couldn't raise much so didn't have any money. All country women did their own sewing and made their own clothes, even before the Depression. But during the Depression, women would use the printed material from the feed sacks or flour sacks to make their dresses. They'd try to buy several sacks of flour in the same print to have enough for a dress.

I went to Ladies Aid one time where ladies were showing off their dresses they had made from flour sacks. They were proud of them. Everybody was in the same boat, you know, nobody had any money. And if they had it, they weren't spending it.

I was going to high school in Lincoln and I had to have fairly nice clothes to go to school in a big city. I had to buy clothes there in Lincoln, because you couldn't get anything very good around where we lived. Mother bought a dress during this time at Penney's in Red Cloud for thirty-seven cents, a plain dress with two holes for arms and a hole for the neck. No trim or anything, just plain material, blue with a little tiny flowered print.

What I bought in Lincoln was a lot better than anything any of the kids in my neighborhood had. I had a red dress with leg of mutton sleeves, silk crepe, tight to the elbow and puffy from the elbow to the shoulder. Mother wanted me to have that dress, she loved red and always wanted me to wear red. I'd wear long hose, neutral rayon hose, and oxfords.

When I went home on holidays and went to church, I felt so embarrassed because my clothes were so much nicer than what the other girls were wearing.

I had a brown dress with buttons on the shoulders at both sides, two or three rows of white silk narrow braid outlining the shoulders. I got it at Miller and Paine in Lincoln. When school started, one of the girls in my class had a dress exactly like mine that she wore on the first day. She was bragging about how she'd gotten that dress in New York, and here I'd gotten mine right in Lincoln at Miller and Paine.

The first year Mother took me shopping and after that, Aunt Bernice would take me. Sometimes I'd look and find things and Aunt Bernice would come see it. She supervised my spending from an account my dad had and she would get money out for me. We'd get our shoes polished in the basement at Miller and Paine for ten cents.

Mother didn't mind spending money on me, but she hated spending it on herself. Her shoes were always kind of worn out.

Dad would say, "You know, Julia, you need to get good shoes."

But she would buy cheap shoes that didn't support her feet well.

Julia Marker

Before the drought, the area got plenty of snow. This road, the mail route, was shoveled out by farmers so the mail car could get through.

CHAPTER FOURTEEN
SEVEN-YEAR DROUGHT

Our neighbors a mile to the south of us sold their cattle for three cents a lb. then held an auction and sold everything. They just walked away from their farm and moved to Bakersfield. Another family four or five miles away did the same thing, and moved to Oregon. Also, that's when my dad's sister Aunt Leone and Uncle Bob left. They were renting, so they just left Nebraska and went to Missouri.

Throughout the area that was the story, sell out and move where there was no drought or dust. But each year, my father and others stayed and kept planting their crops, believing "This year will be better." And each year the dust kept on blowing, and the rains never came.

It wasn't until 1941 that they started having good crops again. It turned out to be a seven-year drought. They experimented with other crops that could grow in dry soil, like milo. '35 and '36 were the driest years, and after that they had a little more rain. When it did rain, there was so much mud because of all the dust. Those were the years that a lot of people moved out because they couldn't raise anything.

Some people didn't have anything to feed the cattle because the drought had dried up the pasture as well as the crops. So then the government bought up the cattle for three or four cents a lb., or $3. for 100 lbs. We heard that the government shot a lot of them. People were saying the government would buy the cattle and then take them out and shoot them.

Because they had a lot of good cattle, Dad and Uncle Ford went up to the sand hill area of Nebraska where it wasn't affected by the drought. They bought an 800 acre ranch where there was a lot of good, green grass for the cattle to graze on. They took their cattle up there, sixty or eighty head of cattle. Dad and Uncle Ford had saved their money through the years, and they were older, not just starting out.

Uncle Ford stayed up there on that ranch the first year. It was a nice farm, with a farmhouse, a barn, a well and everything. He had a couple good riding horses and Catherine and I would go up there and ride around. Dad and Ford's nephew, Milton Lutz, who was Aunt Dora's son, was their hired man. Milton had just gotten married, so he and his wife lived up there with the cattle after the first year, and Ford could come back and take care of his place.

We did keep two or three cows, so we had plenty of milk. We had a garden near our house that we could water with the faucet and hose. So we'd have potatoes, of course, and onions, green beans and tomatoes. That was the main thing.

Uncle Ed from Colorado would get cabbage from neighboring farms, and he'd bring a truckload of cabbage down to get rid of, to sell to people in our community. Mother bought the cabbage and made sauerkraut to keep through the winter. We had plenty of food, not like people in the cities who needed money to buy food. We could live on our garden produce, beef and pork from butchering, chicken, plenty of eggs, milk, butter and cream.

There was a bad-tasting weed that replaced much of the grass in our pasture, and during a couple of summer months the milk became too foul to drink. Even the ice cream we made from that milk tasted awful. The pigs we kept consumed a lot of milk during those dry years, because what we couldn't use we gave to them.

Several of those summers during the Drought, the men didn't have anything to do because there were no fields to cultivate, and they had to get rid of their cattle because there was no pasture. Most of the cattle had all been sold. So when the womenfolk had Ladies Aid, the men would play volleyball. They had a volleyball team and would go around and play teams in other communities.

There were more girls in our community than boys, so the men talked us into having a girls' softball team. We played in a league with other teams in the area. I was a pretty good pitcher. I pitched every game for as long as I could, then when my arm got tired, I played first base.

There were two women in the community who thought we should put on some plays to keep people busy and entertain them. One of the women, Mrs. Brooks, was very literate, a good writer, so she wrote some plays and both women worked to direct them.

One of the plays they bought was called *Here Comes Charlie*. It was about someone named Charlie who was going to come visit an aunt in town, and Charlie turned out to be a girl, a wild tomboy, and all kinds of funny adventures happened when Charlie came. It was performed at the school because of the auditorium. I was in college then, and was one of the young people in the play. I played the aunt. We sold tickets and collected a little money for it, to pay for the purchase of the plays.

One summer about '35 or '36 was such a hot summer. One day I was visiting with my cousin Mildred Holt, who lived in the Norwegian community. She and I were both teaching in country schools by then, and we were always home summers. It was about 126 that day. It was time for noon dinner, and her mother took the butter out of the ice box and set it on the table. When the meal was over, the butter was completely melted, just a pool of yellow in the saucer.

The Markers did alright during the Drought because my dad had saved his money and not gone into debt for anything. He and Mother had grown up the children of homesteaders who had to mortgage the farm to get by, and there was always the fear of losing it if you couldn't pay the mortgage.

Their parents had to work to break up the prairie sod that had never been plowed. Finally they'd get a crop that seemed promising. They looked for a good harvest so they could pay back the money borrowed for seed and machinery. Then a hailstorm would come and destroy their crop. The next year it might be grasshoppers that would darken the sky and eat everything right down to the ground. So another season would pass when they couldn't pay their debt.

My dad was just a boy, but he remembered what that was like and refused to go into debt. His parents had been forced to mortgage the farm to survive, but these were better times. He, and Uncle Ford too, paid for everything as they got it.

But these times were getting to be like the old days. A year or two after the dust storms and the drought started, the grasshoppers came.

One hot day I was standing in the shade of the barn and saw lots of white specks floating along in the sky. A few specks dropped down, and I began to see grasshoppers here and there. That was just the beginning. Soon it was a cloud of grasshoppers that would land and be with us for several years. They chewed up what little there was of the field crops, they chewed the leaves and the bark off the trees. They would even eat bare wood. I saw hundreds of them gnawing away the handle of my dad's pitchfork.

After a year of grasshopper invasion, the county extension office offered farmers a poisoned bran. My dad bought several gunny sacks, and he and I threw handfuls of it on the branches of the pine trees in our yard, hoping to save them. They were our only trees that had survived the drought, as we had watered them with our hose. Our supply of well water depended on the wind blowing the windmill. We had plenty of wind and plenty of well water. We kept the hose running at the base of those trees, changing it about every hour.

One of those summers, our corn was growing real well. My dad hoped to save it from the grasshoppers by using the poisoned bran. He walked down one row, and I'd walk four rows over, carrying the poison bran in large bags over our shoulders and tossing it along the corn rows until the entire field was covered.

My dad and the other farmers who stayed did what they could each year. Finally in 1941, the rains came and they could start growing crops again.

But after the long Drought, it never was the same. So many people had left the area, especially the young people who went elsewhere to earn a living. By then the War was on and many of the young men left to fight overseas. I was one of those who went off to college, then taught school for awhile and did a little traveling.

At Northwestern University in Chicago, I met my future husband. We married September 16, 1944 and settled in Illinois, managing to get back to Nebraska once or twice a year.

In 1949, Bill and I were living in Newman, Illinois. The parsonage had good wood floors, but no rugs. Mother gave us one of her nice wool rugs that she had rolled up during the Dust Bowl days.

After sending it off to the cleaners, I unrolled it and lots of dust settled on the floor as it flapped down. I vacuumed it over and over, front and back, but never could get all the dust out. We used it for awhile, but when we moved to Peoria in 1950, I was glad to get rid of it.

I saw no need to carry along the Nebraska dust. I had my memories of growing up as a Nebraska farm girl, the granddaughter of homesteaders, and those I would always take with me.

Lieten yenta

APPENDIX A:

CHAPTER ENDNOTES

BY LUCILLE MARKER JONES

THE WALSTADS

In 1872, my grandfather Hans Walstad came from Norway to Iowa to Nebraska to become one of the first settlers in Webster County. The Norwegians would come out to Decorah, Iowa, a Norwegian town, and from there travel to various places to settle. My mother always said that her dad, Hans Walstad, was here before George Cather, but they called it Catherton Township just the same.

Jakob and Karen Walstad lived on the Franklin County side and Hans on the Webster County side. The oldest daughter and her husband stayed in Norway, buying the parent's farm for $1000. This is the money that Jakob and Karen brought to America

One large family built a two-story frame house connected to their sod house. This is the only family I knew of who kept the original sod house, as most were glad to get rid of it and build a frame house.

Sofie Walstad lived with us from 1924-26. Mother and Aunt Thilde would each take her for three months at a time. Thilde married Charlie Banks, a Swede, and they lived in the Scandinavian community four miles west of us. Their children were Clarence, Hazel and Stella. When the children got old enough for high school, the parents bought a farm near Inavale. Thilde had a Norwegian accent but not Mother. Mother wanted to be Americanized, and didn't even cook Norwegian.

"Lieten yenta" is Norwegian for "little girl."

THE MARKERS

John Marker, my dad's father, was married to Annie Elizabeth Wilson in Virginia, and they came out to Nebraska with her brothers Clarence, John, Arthur and Albert. The parents and two other married daughters didn't come.

Clarence had two sons and a daughter. His son Ray was superintendent of the church for years and kept it going. John Wilson probably did the best. He gave land for the school house and the New Virginia church.

Aunt Elizabeth, a school teacher, became superintendent of schools in Red Cloud. When she married Will May, they moved to Lincoln and that's where I stayed when I went to high school. Aunt Dora married John Lutz and they lived near Campbell. We always got together with their family at Christmas. After Dora, there was Carrie who married Ed Johnson. They had Cecil, Clayton and Gladys who had Downs Syndrome. Aunt Bernice taught school in Lincoln and never married. After Ford died, Bernice tried to live in their house alone, but ended up in a nursing home in Red Cloud as she had Alzheimers.

THE NEW FARM

My parents had lived on another place with old farm buildings and a little three-room house, but now that they were expecting a child my dad sold cattle and built a nice house. He wasn't a carpenter, he had someone else do the work. My dad kept the old farm and the hired hand lived there and worked the land. Uncle Ford's farm joined ours, so he and my dad often worked together to help each other.

I remember two of the mail carriers, Claude Conley and later Gerald Leonard. Our box was there along with the ones for the Henry Williams and Jay Lovejoy families.

Our fence was woven into long rectangles about an inch and a half wide and six inches long, and curved at the top into scallops. The wire used in this fence was very strong, maybe 1/8" thick.

MOTHER AND ME

During the early years of the Depression, Mother subscribed to the "Comfort" magazine, published in New England. The back half of this magazine contained articles and letters written by subscribers telling about their hobbies. They would tell what they made that they would like to trade for something others had made. Mother would write to women in different states offering to trade an oil painting or a small pastel painting. I remember her receiving salmon from Washington, strawberries from Oregon, embroidered dishtowels and pillowcases, crocheted doilies, etc. One woman in Iowa pieced a quilt for a large oil painting, then Mother sent the quilt top to a woman in South Dakota who quilted it by hand for another oil painting. In fact, my hope chest consisted of dish towels, pillow cases, doilies, that quilt, all things that Mother had received in exchange for paintings.

I didn't care to do embroidery, crochet and so called fancy work. I preferred to read or play outdoors. Mother could do all that but she preferred creating other types of things, like beaded baskets and necklaces, painted winter bouquets from weeds and branches she gathered, plaster of Paris figurines and pictures she would mold, dry and paint. She would have loved ceramics, but back then in the 1920's and 30's she hadn't heard of that.

Mrs. Ellen Lambrecht also usually boarded the schoolteacher. One year when LaVerne Lambrecht was small, he got very sick with pneumonia, and his mother was busy caring for him so the teacher, Gertrude Wiggins, stayed several weeks at our place. We had a hired man, my cousin Milton Lutz, so lots of evenings, my Dad and I and Milton and Miss Wiggins played cards.

MY PRETTY COUSIN CATHERINE

There was some kind of fight later at the stadium, and after that the University of Nebraska never played Notre Dame.

I think one of the reasons I whined and tried to get out of work around the house was because I really didn't feel well much of the time. I had so many allergies and it seemed my nose was always stopped up. I didn't eat right since I was such a picky eater, and was anemic, too. Mother took me to every doctor around, but they all had a different answer as to what my problem was and did nothing to help it.

THE BEST DAD IN NEBRASKA

The lady my mother worked for in Omaha gave my mother a porcelain doll that was slightly broken. The feet were broken off, so Mother made a base for it out of plaster of Paris and kept it for years. This old lady lived in downtown Omaha. Everyone was trying to buy this woman's house and she refused to sell. She had lived there for fifty years, since the Indians were around, and she told my mother about them coming to her door. Back then, this lady said, they didn't dare have a light at night for fear the Indians would see it and come right into the house.

THE NEW VIRGINIA COMMUNITY

I went back in 1981 for the 100th reunion of the New Virginia Church, and that was fun seeing people. I saw Irving Brooks, who was in my class in high school, and he couldn't figure out who I was. They had a program and a dinner, an all day affair, with a church service in the morning, picnic in the afternoon and another church service in the evening. The New Virginia Church was open until just a few years ago in the 1990's, and they stopped services then because there's hardly anyone living out there anymore. The ones who were coming had gotten old or moved away, so it wasn't worth it to pay to keep it open, so they closed it. There's a foundation that wants to keep it in good condition for funerals and weddings, and any community events could be held there. The church is on the Willa Cather tour.

OUR CATHER CONNECTIONS

Albert had come out in 1871 or '72, then his brothers came out around 1876 or '77. There were some Wilson sisters back in Virginia who were married who didn't come to Nebraska, but all the Wilson brothers came. My dad's father, John Marker, had married Lizzie Wilson in Virginia, and my dad was about three when his parents came West.

Jessie Auld and my cousin Stella Fregulia, Mathilde's daughter, were in the same PEO out in Palo Alto, California. Don't ask me what PEO means, only the members know; but it is a service organization for women.

THE BIG CITY

While I was staying at Aunt Elizabeth's, Catherine received a watch from her mother as a birthday present. Oh, I wanted a watch so badly. That was one of the popular fashions of the time, for young people to wear a wristwatch, and I didn't have one. Later, Aunt Bernice gave me one for Christmas, I think it was a Timex, with a leather band. The most popular and nicest watches back then were Elgin. The Elgin watch for girls had a pretty metal wristband. Many students received a good watch as a high school graduation presents, and I got a nice Elgin when I graduated from high school.

An Austin, joked about by the vaudeville team, was a very small car.

DUST BOWL DAYS

I had graduated from high school on January 26, 1934. Back then the city schools had A and B classes. Students could start to school in January as well as September. The B class finished in January. I wasn't in the B class until I was a Senior and had finished all my required subjects and earned extra credits with top grades, so had enough credits to graduate in January. I stayed home with my parents during February and then started in March to Kearney State Teacher's College, which was on the quarter system. I began the third quarter there.

APPENDIX B: WRITINGS (1948-1958) OF JULIA WALSTAD MARKER

Oil painting by Julia Marker

INTERVIEW WITH
THE WORLD HERALD,
OMAHA NEWSPAPER:

Mrs. Julia Marker, whose four hundred acre farm in the middle of Nebraska hasn't produced a spear of grass since 1932, painted her way out of the Depression.

Today Mrs. Marker is proud to announce that her crop of pictures exceeds one thousand, that they have gone to every state in the union and her household budget is balanced.

"We have not had a blade of green grass here for five years," Mrs. Marker said, "so I had to do something. I borrowed a painting and copied it. Since then I have made as many as three oil paintings a day. I send hundreds to stores in Minnesota. I also exchange paintings for embroidery work, quilt tops, oranges from Florida, salmon from Washington, dates from California, and also turkeys from the state of Iowa."

Mrs. Marker said she gets up early in the morning to paint and is often still working at midnight. She never tires, she says, because she loves to paint. She never had any formal art education.

"Only when the dust blows too hard, I have to stop," she explained. "I tried to paint in a dust storm but had to give it up, although I was indoors."

"Sometimes I copy snapshots of animals," Mrs. Marker said. "Sometimes I just copy a picture out of the paper."

"My favorite picture is 'Dog and Lamb,' which I painted in 1934. I also like the one I made of two cranes standing in a stream of water with water lilies in front. I think a picture is more complete with a deer, a dog, bird, or some animal in it."

Mrs. Marker's ambition is to paint a large church mural. "The next time I get an order for a church painting," she said, "I am going to paint a picture of Bethlehem. I want to do a large canvas with lots of color and life. I know I can."

The middle-aged woman who took up painting in lieu of potato planting, makes all her own frames. She augments her income of oil paintings with what she earns from plaster plaques and painting of velvet.

A GIRLS PATH STREWN WITH SNAKES INSTEAD OF ROSES

I have heard of a person's path being strewn with roses, but I never heard of a person's path being strewn with snakes. That happened in my own life so I know it is true. I guess I inherited those snakes from my grandfather and my father. They did their best to rid the country where they lived of snakes, mostly rattlesnakes, by breaking up the sod where the rattlesnakes thrived. But this country has many different kinds of snakes that are not considered poisonous.

I remember seeing rattlesnakes curled up in a coil alongside the road as we walked barefoot to school. I have had blue racers chase me. They are long and slender, a dark blue with head raised a foot above the ground while they wind their way about.

Oil painting by Julia Marker

Watercolor by Julia Marker

One day when I was twelve, herding cattle a mile from home, I saw one of those blue racers. I was curious and got a little too close to it, and when it spied me the race began. I kept turning around while I was running to see the snake still following me, until I got into some tall grass where it lost track of me. And was I glad.

I guess the snakes first took a liking to me as they lay in the windows of our sod house, sunning themselves and watching me when I was a little baby in the cradle. But I think my mother's prayers for my safety kept me from ever being bitten by one. The snakes must have made up their minds that they were going to follow me through life. My path has been strewn with snakes, and it seems that it always will be for I still live in the country.

My folks raised cattle. We milked from ten to twelve cows. We did not have much pasture, so my sister and myself had to herd them in summertime. In winter, they ran in the corn stalk fields after the corn was picked. I went along with my sister when we first started herding on some vacant land that was free for all to herd cattle on. I was four years younger than her, I started herding at the age of eight.

I herded cattle up to the age of twenty. I herded barefoot all through the summer. I went in the ponds while the cattle were grazing. The water seemed so cool on a hot day. I could not swim, but the water wasn't deep. I just waded into the water when suddenly a snake would stick his head up out of the water. I would turn around just to be looking at another snake. I had heard that snakes do not bite in the water, but I wasn't going to stay and find out.

Some summers there were three or four of us girls, each one having their herd of cattle to look after. At noon when

we rounded up the cattle to rest, we went exploring. There
was one place we called snake town where we would go
to look at all the different kinds of snakes. We never missed
seeing one when we made that visit to snake town. I never
dared go there by myself, but when there were four of us I
was brave, even if we saw lots of snakes. Sometimes, we
had a dog along with us.

There was a mad bull in the herd, and one time he got
my sister down in the fence close by our home. I was further back and heard her scream, so I told the dog to hurry
and rescue her. He ran as fast as he could and was soon
there to chase the bull away.

Another time we had a mad bull and, while my mother
and I were milking, the bull came and threw my mother up
in the air with his horns. When she landed on the ground
with the milk all over her, he threw her again. That time
there was no dog around. I took my milk pail and poured
milk all over the bull, then pounded him with it until he let
loose of her. I was twenty when that happened.

My mother lay there helpless on the ground. I chased
the cattle all out of the yard, called my father, and we helped
Mother to the house. She was so heavy we could barely
lift her. She suffered for a whole month. We wanted to get
the doctor, but she would not listen to it. Those days we
had to drive fourteen miles in the lumber wagon to get the
doctor. Her command was law to us. We did not dare call
him when she said no. She was a strong woman and got
through it alright.

I was not afraid of cattle as I spent all my life among
them. I know them and their habits well. I noticed that
when a big fly is buzzing in the air, the cattle will roll their
tails up on top of their backs and start to run. So when it

came time to chase the cattle home, I imitated the buzzing fly until they all had their tails curled up and were running home, their leader in front. The cattle all went in a row, the calves at the end, and me behind them buzzing.

I tried that trick the other day when I chased them home from the stalk field, and it worked after many years and many generations of cattle. They knew what it was, and they all curled up their tails and ran for the barnyard, leaving me alone in the field.

Back to the snakes. They had all kinds of colors of eyes— some red, some green, some yellow. I guess it was the color of those eyes that fascinated me. It would always be the eyes that I'd see first in a snake. While young girls nowadays see all kinds of movies for excitement, I made my own by running away from snakes.

One time we had a cow die of snake bites. The snakes would even follow me at home. We had a bird dog, a long dog with short legs. We had him trained so that when my brother played the accordion the dog would look at his tail and start barking. Then he would take hold of his tail and begin to dance in a circle round and round til everyone got dizzy watching him. The dog got dizzy too, and would fall like a drunk person right down on the floor, which would cause us all to roar with laughter. People came from miles to see him perform this wild dance that only happened when my brother played the accordion

I worshiped that dog. One day there was a snake close to the house, and I urged the dog on him. My mother said it was only a grass snake, but it proved poisonous for it killed our dog Trip. He would sit there for days with his head swelled up, and watch me through swollen, accusing eyes. When he died I felt like I had lost a good friend, and it was all my fault.

Another time we had a dog fighting a snake. The dog got out of it alright, but it wasn't so good for me as he threw the snake right down at my feet. It curled up my leg clear to the knee. I gave a kick and a jump to throw it some distance.

With my hand I have felt a cold snake on a hen's nest. My brother killed it, and afterward we could see it was a five foot long bull snake.

In the drought years I wanted lily pools. We had several in the yard. The ponds were all dry and there was no water for the snakes, so they soon found my lily pools. Once when I opened the screen door, one flopped right down by my feet. Another time, one was hanging on the screen door. One got in the basement, and we killed it.

I got rid of all the lily pools, filling them up with dirt, so that problem was settled. We didn't get any rain all summer and had to water the garden with a hose. The snakes soon found that out. As I was hoeing weeds out of the garden, I saw a snake rubbing his head against the softness of my shoes, with his greenish eyes looking right at me. I stood paralyzed for a moment. I could see his long body in the weeds. My husband heard me scream and came and killed the snake.

Snakes are good rat killers so sometimes we let them go. Last summer while tearing up the floor of a corn crib, we found two of the large snakes crawling in the rat holes. They eat rats in the nest. With a spade in one hand while tearing up the floor, whenever I saw a rat, I'd put the spade down quick and cut it in two. I killed seventeen rats in one day.

The farm is not always such a pleasant place to live. We have gone through drought, and grasshoppers that would take whole fields of corn when it was ready to tassel. I have seen swarms of grasshoppers that were so thick they hid the sun like a cloud, and buildings covered with hoppers so that the walls looked black. They ate the bark off trees, they even ate the handle off a pitchfork. They quickly finished the corn so that there was not a green straw or a green leaf left. It looked like the ground had just been plowed.

Along with the grasshoppers and the drought, I remember one of the worst dust storms in history that followed a dry, windy winter. People got lost on the road or in their own yards. It started at eight p.m. and kept on all night. In the house we had to sit with wet cloths over our faces so we could breathe.

People would come from other states and cry, they felt so sorry for the people in this community. I never traveled any in those days and did not realize that fifty or one hundred miles away they had rain and snow and no dust storms. We managed to live through it all as we had cattle, just a few, and chickens, also a hog to butcher. All feed had to be shipped in.

The next spring, we didn't have much rain but enough to stop the dust storms. Out west sixty or more miles they had floods. The Republican River came like a wall, overflowing bottom farm lands which had not suffered from drought like we had. Lots of people were drowned. Some were saved by climbing trees. They said the snakes and rats also climbed the same trees. The snakes climbed clear to the tops while the rats were not so decent, and the people had to fight the rats for space in the trees. I was down to see the river as it came like a wall ten to twelve feet high, overflowing towns along the river. We could hear it roar nine miles away where we lived on high ground. I saw people using boats on the streets, while we on the hills could cultivate corn. But it got so dry for us that summer that we just raised fodder with no corn on it.

I never knew what it was to go to movies or play bridge. People on the farm have to work hard. In summertime, we eat breakfast at 6 a.m. and supper as late as ten. Farmers can never strike. They put in crops every year and lots of time they do not raise enough to pay for the seed. Living nine to fourteen miles from the nearest towns, we only get there once a week. In winter, when snow drifts are piled high on country roads, we always get the worst of it. This year we could not get to town for five weeks, while a few miles from here they could go everyday. Mail did not come, phone was out of order, radio wouldn't work.

We have plenty of wind, so a windcharger furnishes us with electricity which runs our radio, washing machine, iron, fan and lights. Wind also runs the windmills which furnish water for the stock and the home. It fills our supply tank in the basement.

For amusement, I always have to make my own, because I can never get to town when there is a good movie there. The dirt roads are always wet and slippery, or filled with snow. So I have just managed to see three good movies–"One Foot in Heaven," "How Green is my Valley," and "Gone With the Wind."

Having plenty of time since Lucille, our only child, left for high school, then University and teaching school, now married to a minister and living in Illinois, I have to keep busy to keep from being lonely. So with my husband busy in the field, I built chicken houses. One time I had one finished and was sitting on the floor putting a window in it. There was the everlasting snake lying stretched out on the floor watching me. I never can get away from snakes, even in my dreams.

The only time they do not bother me is when I climb the ladder and paint the buildings, which I used to do every three or four years. I used to paint them all by myself. Painting the barn I climbed an eighteen foot ladder, had a six foot handle on my paint brush, and I got it painted clear to the top. I also climbed the same ladder and painted our two story house clear to the top. The other buildings, like the granary, corn cribs, hog house, ice house and garage were not so high. I used to paint them all, many a time.

I have lived on this farm twenty-nine years, but I have let up some and started to paint only the lower half of the buildings and had the other half done by a painter. I papered the rooms every other year, also did this by myself. I had help only the first time I papered them. I have taken the car and gone three miles to get sand mixed with cement and cemented floors in chicken houses and bins.

This is the way one woman spends her time on the farm. Living close to nature and to the snakes seems to agree with me. I have always been strong and undertook to do anything I felt like.

THE DUST BOWL

There are so many people who cannot even imagine what the "dust bowl" looked like. It was a place that seemed like God had forsaken it. Some said, "The people were too wicked, they were paying for their sins." I was sitting in

our church one time during dust storm years and heard
these very words.

My mind dwelt on first one then another in the community, but they all seemed like respectable people. Why
there was hardly a one in this dust bowl neighborhood who
smoked or drank whiskey, or even beer. They were
hardworking farmers who year after year prepared the soil
and planted corn and wheat, with high hopes every year,
hoping they had seen the last of it. They were standing the
drought, but debt piled up. Some summers there was not
even a green straw. The worst was the spring when the
first big dust storm came.

After that, grasshoppers destroyed every bit of growing vegetation. We stood and looked at the swarm of grasshoppers that clouded the sun and was black like a rain cloud
with moving elements in it.

During the dust bowl, we rolled up the mattresses every morning as we got up, so the bed would not get full of
dust. Through the window it looked like a black snow-
storm. We had to have lights on in the daytime. Those that
lived so far from town like we did would not even venture
to go the fourteen miles to get our supply. It seemed that
we lived on almost nothing sometimes. We got so tired of
eggs we could hardly stand the sight of them.

One spring the flood came. It was eight miles from
where we lived, and we could hear the roar of the river.
We just had a little shower, enough to lay the dust. The
river was doing its destruction, and many people drowned.
Some would climb up in the trees. Those that survived
said that rats and snakes also would climb up in the same
tree. The snakes didn't pay any attention to the others in

the tree, but not so with the rats. They tried to bite the people up there.

Nothing was raised in '36 as the grasshoppers were worse than the year before. They came back every summer until 1942. Now we see one once in awhile.

There were lots of young people in the community during the drought years. But they all went away to college and universities. They almost all left the farms and either taught school or got a job in the city, which left the older folks alone on the farm. Then the old folks also moved to town, leaving many farm homes vacant. Farm homes disappeared one by one. Some were torn down, others moved their house to the nearest town to live in.

A SOD HOUSE

Most any kind of a dwelling house can be replaced except a sod house. They are gone forever and there is only the memory left, which is still fresh in my mind. It was one of the nicest homes I ever had, and the first house my parents built after the dugout days.

Father broke the sod. After hooking the oxen to the breaking plow, he selected the buffalo grass ground on the prairie where the toughest sod was. It couldn't be too close to the buffalo wallows where water was standing to form little lakes on the prairie. He had to be on the lookout for rattlesnakes that would often times wind themselves up on the breaking plow. Father always wore boots to protect his feet from their poisonous bites. He oftentimes carried a gun on the plow. One time he forgot the gun and pulled off his boot to kill a snake.

The sod was a foot wide. They cut it with a spade into two foot lengths. They used a platform on the running gear of the wagon to load it on. Father unloaded the sod while Mother built the wall, laying the sod like brick with the grass side down. They did not break up more sod than could be used in one day, because the sod was not so good to handle after it got wet.

Three feet thick walls made nice windows for raising flowers, especially geraniums which are loaded with blossoms the year round. I never will forget one time I came home from school and saw the Minister kneeling outside the sod house window. I wondered if something had happened to Mother, that perhaps he was kneeling down praying for her, when the door opened and Mother appeared. The Minister, still kneeling and unable to speak, just pointed to the flowers crimson with blooms and as high as the window.

How nice it was when Mother whitewashed the walls, how clean and refreshing the room looked. This she did after almost every rain. The sod on the roof did not keep it from leaking. Mother used to sit in bed and hold the umbrella over my sister and I when it rained.

Living on the prairie is so close to nature, and the air is refreshing, a good place for children to roam around and make all the noise they want and not disturb the neighbors.

There was a rope swing in the barn where we could swing for hours, the wheelbarrow to ride in when older children would pull it. If we wanted anything to eat, we went down along the creek and picked all the wild plums, grapes and chokecherries which grew wild.

For many years we never saw town, the folks went in the lumber wagon. It took all day. The dog started to watch for them early in the afternoon and never moved, but kept a steady watch. When he saw them coming over the hills several miles away, he started out to meet them.

Mother always brought us a nickel's worth of candy, which we were glad to get. We never entertained very much, we went over two miles to school, which we enjoyed. There were children of different nationalities. At first we had a time to understand one another. The teacher sure had a time of teaching us all to speak the American language plus writing and reading.

Our folks really started to enjoy the homestead they had worked so hard to improve. They now had large corn fields, also wheat did well when we had rain. They now had a permanent home where they could spend their last days without fear of losing it.

On the prairie there was no noise except for the dogs barking and the wolves howling at night. Sometimes the sunset is in the north, east or south, a freak of nature caused by a cloud obscuring the sun so it throws the rays from the side. The beautiful sunsets in red and lavender, so much color that if an artist had painted them, I would say he sometimes used too much red and too bright lavender.

EARLY SETTLERS-- THE HOMESTEADERS

In the summer of the early 1870's, my father and a number of others decided to go to the plains of Nebraska to take a homestead on which they would have to live five years, when they would then become the owner of the land and get the deed to it. Some had worked as carpenters in the larger cities, my father being one of them. Others had worked in lumber camps and saw mills. They were all hard-working men and had the strength to face the hardships of the Wild West.

They had saved most of the money they made and were buying necessities for the trip. A span of oxen and a covered wagon were the first things purchased. There was always someone ready with advice on what to take along when going west. A gun, they said, was necessary to protect yourselves from the Indians. In the East, they thought the Indians were standing at every corner, ready to attack the immigrants as they came through.

After they purchased the necessities, which comprised a gun, a breaking plow, spade, some carpenter tools, food, cooking utensils, extra clothing, a few blankets to sleep on and whatever else they thought they needed, they joined the steady stream of covered wagons going West.

There were quite a few Norwegians and other nationalities who could not understand so much of the American language. My father had come from Norway in 1869 and settled in Norwegian communities like Decorah, Iowa, but there were others who had been in the United States longer and had gone to school here and learned to write beside. They could also translate to the Americans, and they were a real help to those who knew so little about the United States.

Some intended to settle in the eastern part of Nebraska. Others decided to go on to Colorado. My father wanted to go to the western part of Nebraska. They could only travel from ten to twenty miles a day and had to stop often to let the oxen rest and graze. While they were resting, the men took their guns and went for a hunt. There was lots of wild game, prairie chicken, rabbits, wild ducks and geese. Sometimes when they were close to a stream, the wild game became more plentiful as they came further west. They even shot wild turkeys along the river. They roasted some of these birds on an open fire they made by digging a hole in a bank and putting a grate over it. Some rubbed mud all over the roast real thick and left it right in the fire for several hours. When they peeled that hard crust off, they had some of the finest roast they had ever eaten.

They crossed the Missouri on a ferry boat. When they came to other rivers, they sometimes had to wait around a day or two if it was after a heavy rain and the stream was swollen. They did not dare to cross until after it went down.

The trees disappeared entirely as they came further west. The country looked so bare, until at last there was not a tree or house in sight, just the endless plains covered with buffalo grass and yellow cactus in full bloom. Some wanted to settle where there was a creek with trees, and grass for the oxen.

At last they came to such a place. It was a hot day in the late summer. The trees shaded the water in the creek that looked so cool. There were grape vines on the trees, and they were covered with wild grapes that were still green. There were also plum trees that were loaded with plums.

There was also a trading post ten miles south of where some of the homesteaders were, but no railroad within forty to sixty miles. There were some places seventy miles or more between the railroads running east and west. They had a stagecoach going between these places to the country store, carrying passengers and mail, but the homesteaders did not get any mail for a whole month. When they had to go to the country store for some supplies, they often walked. It would take them about as long to walk as to drive, since the oxen were very slow.

They used the water from the creek, as some were without a well for several years. They carried their drinking water from a neighbor that had a well. Wells were not easily made as it was over a hundred feet to water.

One man dug the well with a spade. They had a wooden box that went down in the hole, and as he dug the dirt he put it in the box, which was hoisted up and emptied. When the well digger had it full of dirt, he pulled on the rope to signal that the box was ready to be pulled up. The one that dug the well would go from place to place and dig wells. Some were two hundred feet down. They had to lower a tubing as he went down. There were no rocks here on the plains. There was black dirt down about two feet and clay until they got down to about sixty feet.

Wells here in Nebraska never go dry. This state has more rivers than any state, and the water here comes from the supply in the northern part, which is a sandy country. Closer to the river it is not so far down to water. There are even springs which always supply cool, fresh drinking water.

The early settlers struggled on and kept breaking up more sod, and plowed it the next year and planted a few acres corn with a hand planter. They bought a milk cow which was larietted for years before they could get a pasture. They got a hog the year after they came and dug a hole in the ground two to three feet deep so the hog could not get out. They built a shed in one end which was some poles with brush over. They also got some chickens. The chicken house was another dugout, but there were no rats or skunks those days that took chickens. It was just clay walls and floor. Sometimes snakes would disturb the chickens.

A few times they had some buffalo meat, but there were not many buffalo left in the country. They had gone west to the Rockies, as did the deer, elk and antelope. And the Indians went behind following their trail. The Indians were always hunting the buffalo. They could ride their ponies faster than the buffalo could run, and with their bow and arrow, they had killed many a buffalo before the white man ever came to this country. Many an arrow was plowed up by the early settlers, some still in good condition. How long the Indians had been here no one could tell as they did not farm the country, only hunted all the time and camped by the river. Even in these later years, there has been many a burial ground found where the Indians were buried.

But the rattlesnakes stayed on for many years. They would be winding around the poles under the roof of the dugout. The settlers had their guns ready to shoot them at a moment's notice.

The stove pipe run up through the dugout roof, and the only sign of life was when the smoke would come out of the bank. The pioneers felt a sense of peace and security in this wide open space in the country, with the sky filled with sparkling stars. Sometimes on a moonlit evening, the coyotes would look like dogs, racing over the prairie in the night and hiding behind the shadows of the tall grass.

The buffalo seemed to scent the approach of the white man and fled in advance. In the earliest days, the buffalo were so plentiful that the settlers supplied themselves as far as they could with buffalo meat. The settlers of 1870 saw more buffalo and had more experience with them. Sometimes along the river, people would stand on top of the bluffs and look down on thousands of buffalo grazing along the river. When the herd left for another grazing place across the river, they crossed it one by one until they were all on the other side, with antelopes and wolves traveling with them. The antelopes were not so wild and were very curious. They liked to see what the people were doing and would stand and watch the log houses being built.

The hardships were almost unbearable in the earlier years for settlers who had taken homesteads in the eastern counties of Nebraska. The Indians would kill and rob the people, so when the settlers dug their dugout, they also made a ditch from there to the creek. Then they could go unobserved by incoming Indians and get water.

For those who had lived in the city, it took years to get used to this life. I have heard some of the older women say they went down by the creek to sit under a tree and cry while they sewed. The boys liked a life full of adventure, killing rattlesnakes and cutting off the rattlers to see how many they could get and shooting wild game.

The early settlers could get an elk or a deer down by the river. They could watch the Indian women cutting wood, putting the papoose down beside the tree while they worked. They carried the firewood high on their heads and carried the papoose on their backs.

In the summer of 1874, grasshoppers invaded Nebraska. They were the Rocky Mountain grasshoppers and came in swarms from the West. They were so numerous they looked like great clouds that darkened the sun. The vibration of their wings filled the air with a roaring sound. All corn was eaten in a single day, nothing remained but the stumps. They ate potatoes and onions, even dug the earth away so they would be sure to get it all, leaving just the peelings of the onions. It was hard to drive a team across a field because the grasshoppers flew up with such force, they struck the horses in the face. Chickens feasted on the grasshoppers but there were plenty left to do damage.

Most of the settlers were very poor and lived on their sod corn and garden. Now these were all gone, and it looked like starvation. Some sold or gave away their claims and went back East. Others would take their teams and go to older settlements to find work. The rest stayed and hunted wild game. They would go out on the prairie in their covered wagons and pick up buffalo bones. When they got a load they took them to the nearest railroad town which took two days travel. The bones were sold in exchange for cornmeal that was used to make bread.

Thus the hard winter of 1874-1875 was lived through. Those were the darkest days in the history of the western pioneers. Those that left their claims wished many times they had stayed because it got better after that. They all needed help those days in one way or another. Their aim was to improve the whole community to a better way of life, and they came up with new ideas to store food and insure health to everyone.

A blacksmith shop was built in a bank with a sod front. Grandfather Jakob Walstad had some experience in Norway in that line of work. People would come there and he would help them to do their own black smithing.

This sod shop had a cave underneath it and was very steep and cool. It was tunneled in under the floor, very cool in the summer and used for storing food. The shop had been in use for several years when one day a two-year-old steer was grazing in the pasture near this dugout. He went on top of the roof and fell through, landing in the blacksmith shop. He didn't stop there, but went right in through the shop and landed in the cave. The neighbors had to come with rope and tackle. This they fastened on the pole which was top of the shop and they lowered it down and fastened it around the steer, and pulled him up without a scratch. After that, a fence was made around the roof where it was even with the ground.

It seemed like in those days, everyone depended on their neighbors.

Granddaughter of homesteaders

APPENDIX C:

ADDITIONAL PHOTOGRAPHS

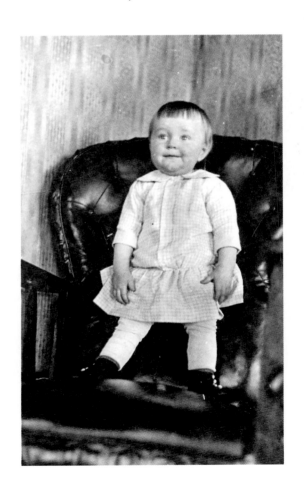

John and Julia by front porch of home, 1920

The Marker farmhouse

Lucille at Christmas, 1918

Grainary with windcharger

District 66 Schoolhouse Julia Walstad attended as a child

Shelling grain

Threshing oats and wheat

At the Inavale Depot, 1935, after the dam on the Republican River broke during the night, flooding farmland and houses, killing a hundred people while they slept.

Mr. and Mrs. William C. Jones, September 16, 1944

John Marker with his first granddaughter, 1946

Lucille with daughters at Thanksgiving, 1954

The Jones family camping, 1958

Lucille and daughter Karen, Aitkin, Minnesota, March 2007